I0167592

THE

GATECRASHER

Historical steps on how Donald John Trump gatecrashed the political machines of Bush, Clinton and Obama to win the presidency in 2016, more than fire and furious, and better explained than hacking.

ZENTS K. SOWUNMI

For additional copies of this or other Zents Sowunmi titles write:

Korloki Publishers Inc, Brooklyn, New York 11230

Please allow 4 to 6 weeks for delivery. For bulk orders contact us via email

Korlokipublishers@gmail.com

THE

GATECRASHER

Inside historical journey on how
Donald Trump destroyed the political machines
of Bush, Clinton and Obama to win the Presidency

ZENTS K SOWUNMI

Don't miss these exciting books from

bestselling   Author

ZENTS KUNLE SOWUNMI

- ❖ *The Vultures and Vulnerable*
- ❖ *President Obama: Hero or villain of Capitalism?*
- ❖ *Unequally Yoking*
- ❖ *Ogun State Policy of Manipulation.*
- ❖ *Before the Journey Became Home*
- ❖ *100 ways to Laugh*
- ❖ *Cien Maneras de Reir*
- ❖ *What happened to Our Democracy?*
- ❖ *Not a stranger Anymore*

Coming soon!!!

- ❖ **The Loopholes**
- ❖ **The mischievous Widow**
- ❖ **The Covenant Breakers**
- ❖ **The Secret of Gabriel**

Order copies of this author's books directly from www.kpcbooks.com

Cover design by:	Korloki Publishers Inc.
Interior design:	Korloki Publishers Inc.
Photographs:	Zents K Sowunmi
Summary:	Political, thriller and suspense life story of POTUS Donald John Trump

ISBN: 9781936739363

ISBN: 1936739364

PRINTED IN UNITED STATES OF AMERICA

AUTHOR OF THE VULTURES

&

VULNERABLE

ZENTS SOWUNMI

A POLITICAL NOVEL OUT OF CURIOSITY

KORLOKI: An imprint of Korloki Publishers Inc Brooklyn

New York 11230

DEDICATION

To my mother

Late Hannah Sowunmi

THE

GATECRASHER

Resounding praises for the Oracle

International Best Selling

Author

Zents Sowunmi

A Super story maker and a teller of our time

Dr. **Adeyemi**   Lagos Nigeria

His ability to bring the story to your door step is exceptionally unique.

Jacky Vasquez, Brooklyn NY

The Oracle Zents is quite a spot to read.

Dauda Shokeye Bronx NY

A master at mixing reality of our time with fiction

Lanre Tejuosho Maryland MD

Creative and daring.

Susan Anderson, Dallas Texas

ZENTS

SOWUNMI

KORLOKI: AN IMPRINT OF KORLOKI PUBLISHERS INC.

The Beginning

Π

Before the Move:

By the end of 2012 President election which Barack Obama won, it was apparent if the Republicans did not regroup and listen more to the noise and anxiety of the Tea Party, the nature of the national politics was heading for another eight years if not more of Democrat values with global thinking and the nation may witness a physical war not only on the 1789 Constitution, hut on gradual imposition on foreign ideologies on a nation based on Christian values.

President Obama deported more immigrants than his predecessors, about two million were deported mostly from Africa, the birth place of his father, Obama Senior, he promoted his open support for refugees mostly from the Muslims countries than those from Christian countries, and his views on the future of the country on diversity threatened the status quo of the White Americans, the Coal miners in all the 25 states for his global warming stuff and the positions of the Evangelicals, his presidency was too friendly with ideas not in consonance with the traditional values of America on LGBT, the Muslims, and traditional jobs of the coal miners in over 25 states in America.

Another term of Democrats in the White House was ready not only to destroy the Constitution, it was ready to change the judiciary system, as all the circuits court judges were almost all appointees of President Obama, the Supreme Court Justices were almost within the control of the Democrat Party after the death of Justice Scalia, everything was pointing to a nation of one party system if care or drastic approach was not undertaken.

The war to save the Republican Party was not what the traditional, soft spoken politicians could undertake, political correctness dominated their thinking rather than facing the reality, every group within the Republican Party expressed fear or lived in fear of tomorrow in which all the Whites would be minority, their history will be history, their positions in the society would be lost, and many may have to re-read the books on Columbus and relocate to another country or planet.

President Bush and his father both former Republican Presidents had been compromised, the Clinton knew their weaknesses, he made them family friends, he knew if he could get the Bush family, he could get the conservatives to see Hillary his wife as a future Presidential material. It was why he became a virus into the lives of the Bush families, he had fix that of the Blacks when he relocated his office to Harlem New York and his residency in Chappaqua in the outskirt of New York.

An outsider like Donald J Trump of New York with no political future at stake, or legacy to protect, and probably with nothing to lose, became the Idea candidate not only to checkmate the global thinking and direction of the Democrats from the already laid down plan in the last 25 years, he would with his sharp tongue fight the war with all he had.

The move

I was waiting for my next move in my little Apartment on Carpenter Avenue in Bronx, New York in December 8, 2009, with just one year of living in New York City and several years in Texas, the much-awaited call finally came with his deep voice.

Major Charles Quick, the Director, of Rehab Center, of the William Beaumont Army Medical Center El Paso Texas came on the line, the avalanche of wounded soldiers needed to go through a program under the Warrior Transition Battalion, and my services was needed.

I was never a reserved military personnel, never had a gun and just wondered why and how my name came up in the data base of United States Department of Defense and it was still a strange development to me, however, my years with the Army Hospital in El Paso, Texas, a border town to Mexico and subsequent transfer to full time position as Warrior Transition Coordinator with WTB Fort Bliss Texas prepared my orientation to understand the thinking and frustration of the United States Military man and women with Obama's Presidency.

Most of the soldiers believed President Obama made the US Military weaker and less adventurous, they witnessed massive budget military cuts since Jimmy Carter, it was the general opinion of the men in Uniform and as years went by.

I realized they made me to understand America more than the sweet-talk of the Harvard Law Professor Barack Obama or that of President Bill Clinton which I had been fascinated with in the last 15 years.

It got clearer to me.

At the same time, it never occurred to me in future, I would write a book on the believe system of the conservatives or that of the unusual 2016 Presidential candidate, Donald J Trump after my book on President Barack Obama *"The Hero or villain of Capitalism?"* In which Obama's election as 44th President of the United States America in 2008 brought tears of joy across the globe.

However, it happened, in 2017 as an African American, we have been conditioned in politics to reason that being a Black American, Democrat Party must be one's first choice, and secondly, only a traitor to the goals of American Americans would be a Republican, as details of American history were hidden from us, particularly, the first generation African Americans.

The Liberal Press, and civil right lawyers and writers made it possible to see the Republican Party as evil and unfriendly to the Blacks, unfortunately, the truth would only be left to those who could read and search for information, not some porous minded individuals.

It was the way the politics of America was set up since 1960 when late President Kennedy, a Democrat switched the loyalty of the African Americans from the Republican Party to that of his Party with the controversial Presidential result with less than two hundred thousand votes to win the presidency.

Then Vice President, Richard Nixon had the opportunity to contest the rigged figures in Chicago in the favor of JFK, but he did not, it was how Democrat Party became the home for the African Americans in politics and socio affiliations.

And several decades of loyalty to the Republican Party since Abraham Lincoln who freed the blacks as slaves up to President Eschewer in 1960 was erased and African Americans threw the Republican Party under the bus, or what can it be called?

Since then, it was difficult to convince average African Americans that Republican Party was ever a friend in the past and even in the present and gradually, it never occurred to those who cared to find the truth particularly the new immigrants from all over the world, the United States of America must always be greater than the Party they belong, and it should be all about the Constitution, the Philadelphia document since 1789.

To cement the loyalty to its ideas of over dependents, the Democrats embarked on massive social benefits which eventually crippled the new generation and African Americans, and when Sean Combs known as Puff Daddy or Puff Diddy saw how the eight years Obama presidency went faster without anything of significance change in his people, his lamentation was welcomed, "we have been shortchanged with the so-called Black President" were his words.

Puff Daddy got most of us thinking, including some black Church leaders as 39 percent of those in jail were Blacks, 58 percent unemployed youths, number one in school dropouts, and most of the students were not interested in Mathematics and English Language, and crime rates became more of concern to the people than the presidency and later in years to come, 3-6 million African Americans women never have husband or boyfriends. What went wrong?

Among the Whites, they too faced economic challenges as their income was shrinking and taxes imposed by the Federal, states and Cities in almost everything too burdensome, just to sustain the welfare programs of the Democrats and years of senseless wars of the past Republican administration of the last two Bush presidency. It was no longer a smiling issue.

For the first time, most of the affected middle-class Americans affected by the economic down turn unashamedly filed for unemployment benefits and working was no longer based on dignity, it became a passion for the fools and the recipients of food stamps went up to 47 million from 27 million during Obama's administration.

With the above political playground, the Republican Party candidate for 2016 Donald J Trump with candor took oxygen out of the political room in America, he was like a movie star, who never shared the glamor of every scene with any other characters, he controlled every step of it to the end.

Without Donald Trump, it would be right to assume 2016 Presidential elections would have been lifeless; with "low energy" Jeb Bush calling the shot, or "Lying" Ted telling Americans how conservative he was, even the Ohio State Governor John Kasich and others Trump gave names, the primaries would have been too carefully regulated.

However, Trump brought life into it with his mouth like motivational totality of a warrior, more like the Rambo or Rocky fame of the eighties. It was not even Donald Trump's mouth alone or words that got my attention, far from it, it was the way he made average Americans, at least those who listened to him, to feel selfishly proud again, he pumped oxygen into it with his massive weight and standalone hair style on his head, he made them to see the ugly picture of events around them. He gave hope where it was almost gone. It was nothing but the exceptionality of America he preached.

Trump's messages were clearer and precise like that of a car salesman much more than the lifeless and helpless messages of all his rivals from primaries to the actual election. He was special and different, with his massive height of 6.2" and show-like presentations unlike what the American voters had seen in the past. He became a product of interest to everyone, not even to his country, he was the same candidate people of all races all over the globe glued to the television to see and hear.

Every night, in all the corners of the world, everyone switched on the cable networks just to hear him, it would not be wrong to assume that CNN a Liberal Station with interest in the Democrat Party made lots of money on Trump, as their viewership exploded in millions, they focused more on his shortcomings than his messages, with that, they misled millions all over the world.

In all the Mosques, all other the world, Trump became the guy the Islamic nations got scared off since the end of Ottoman Empire, they conducted special prayers (tabatadah) on him, they wanted him to lose the election, they all wanted him to fail, it would the first time somebody with balls called them names openly.

He did.

Trump wanted the immigration statues of all Muslims in America reviewed, the Hispanics were scared to their pants, their increasing population was about to be checkmated by a President tougher than Ronald Reagan, with several hundreds of Muslim Centers all over the country, it was almost clash of faith and survival of the White race.

It was funny, Trump promised America a border wall against Mexico in the down South and he wanted the country of Mexico to pay for it and in fear they walked around.

In Africa continent, it was a mixed feeling, as camps broke up between the Muslims and Christians, the Muslims in Africa viewed his policies with hatred, they joined hands in circulating fake news against his personality and his words were negatively embellished The Christians however, felt relieved, maybe Trump will be the Biblical Daniel to check the encroachment of Islam into traditional areas of the Christian world, may be.

However, only the Asians were at peace with themselves as they watched the political journey of candidate Trump to the White House with interest as if they had prepared for the outcome well in advance good or bad.

Candidate Trump used all the positives and negatives to embellish the narratives around his listeners to describe his messages. He was straight to the point in most cases, with funny captivating gestures.

When Trump mentioned how eighty thousand companies left the United States of America for overseas due to heavy taxes as high as 35%, NAFTA, (North America Free Trade Act) signed by President Bill Clinton in the nineties as one of the reasons for job theft in the country and World Trade signed deals of the previous administration in the nineties which were all true, if not, what happened to all the empty factories all over the nation?

Donald Trump mentioned how Islam as a religion from the Middle East was a threat to western civilization, if his words were lies, what about the Allah Akbar messages from terrorists before their diabolical acts?

The radical Islamic attacks in San Bernardino California, and Florida were still fresh in the memories of all, or the endless attacks on Americans and Israel from radical Islamic nations particularly Iran?

When candidate Trump highlighted the failures of former President Obama foreign policy in North Africa, in nations like Libya which led to the death of Col Mummer

Gadhafi and four Americans including Ambassador Stephens, the loss of American traditional influence in Egypt since the time of President Jimmy Carter in the seventies, it was too much of a failure to comprehend as American watched with disgust how Russia took over the legacy of Jimmy Carter in Egypt.

Russian President Vladimir Putin official visit to Cairo in February 9th, 2015 was a big thing on CNN, BBC, Aljazeera, and most news media worldwide, it attracted red carpet treatment from General Sissi who took over after the removal of the conservative and radical President Morsi and suspension of economic benefits accrued to the Pharaoh's country by Obama's administration since the era of Jimmy Carter.

Furthermore, Wall Street Journal reporter, Jay Solomon in his book" *The Iran wars*" told MSNBC that President Obama back out of the Red line because of his determination to close the deal with Iran, however, the so-called Red line failure became a problem for him to keep his promise in Syria to the Rebels against Dictator President Basher al- Assad of Syria which led to uncontrollable increase in the refugees' movement mostly Muslims into Western nations, Trump got his messages across faster.

Refugees incursion to the Western World was more than just moral obligation, it was indeed an export of Islamic religion into the hearts and might of Western Civilization based on the fundamentals and values of Christianity, the only religion that could be a threat to Islam.

Furthermore, Donald J Trump in his introductory stage had called the Mexicans names as a group of people bringing drugs, rapists and criminals to America or how he disputed the heroism of Senator John McCain a 2008 GOP nominee for President, it was very astonished, I felt his adversaries finally got him and never knew if he was ever going to survive it, but he did.

McCain was a prisoner of war in North Vietnam, his war injury however left him permanently incapable of raising his hand above his head for five and half years until his release on March 14th 1973, no one understood Senator John McCain's politics not even his fans, they called him mavericks, however, they respected his contributions to the nation, the fear of those who got scared with his utterances assumed that if the nation was left alone to Senator McCain, the United States of America would be at war with more than eight nations at the same time, somehow, one would think, he had nothing but war to offer the nation.

Senator John McCain (81) from the state of Arizona tried to turn the table of attack back to Trump with a link to all to all Veterans but he had no likeable reputation with the mainstream Press who saw how he destroyed most of the President Obama programs, the President who defeated him in 2008 election.

The Press ignored John McCain particularly on Morning Joe show on MSNBC and both Co-hosts Mika Brzezinski and Joe Scarborough had a good laugh every morning. CNN was happy too and all of them owned by the Liberal money men with influence had no feelings for the sentiments expressed by the Senator, late President Reagan pleaded for in the earlier stage of his political career, to them, Trump would be an easy target for their candidate Hillary Clinton and they were ready to tag along the endless journey that eventually destroyed their hopes for Hillary Clinton.

However, Donald Trump's war against McCain and the establishment he attacked would not be his wars alone, it would be a difficult task for him to confront, two political dynasties, of Clinton and Bush and two terms sitting President Barack Obama, along with the biased mainstream media and social media. It was never going to be an easy task for the gatecrasher into the exclusive political territories controlled by the Bushes, Clintons, Obama and establishment forces for decades.

What Donald Trump had as his political weapons were what eventually inspired this book and with the hope readers would understand the wars against the establishment he mentioned throughout the campaign and several years into his presidency.

This book would cover the road to his Presidency and first year in office, challenges and if his first term would scale through the obstacles on his ways by his adversaries.

Thank you.

12/25/2017

(1)

BEFORE 2016

Donald John Trump was an unusual person from Queens New York, about 6.2 feet tall, who got his upward life movement from a father with a German blood. His grandfather Frederic Trump born in Kallstadt in the United Kingdom of Bavaria, who at the age of 16 years migrated to the United States of America started life career as a Berber, several years later, he moved to Northwest and made his fortunes in restaurant business and boarding houses.

Trump's grandfather, did not live long, he died at the age of 49 years in 1918 in Woodhaven Queens New York, but he left his son Frederick Chris Trump, the father of Donald J Trump to continue his legacy of hard work.

As a kid, Donald Trump spent the first four years of his life in a five-bed room Tudor, located at 85-15 Wareham place Jamaica Estates Queens New York, the home was built by his father and of recent as March 2017, it was sold for $2.14million.

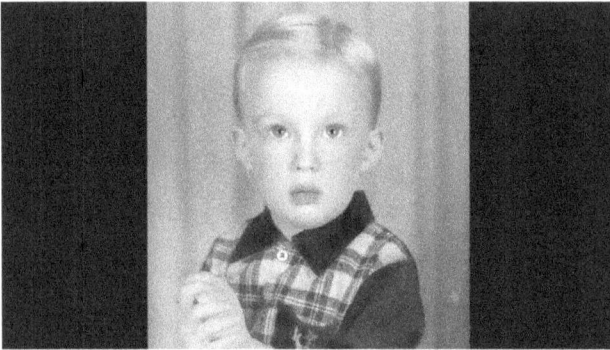

Future President of America Donald J Trump

However, Frederic Chris Trump Snr was an American real estate developer and philanthropist, primarily in Brooklyn New

York, born in October 1905, in Woodhaven, New York City. He took his son, the future President of the United States of America into real estate business at early stage and by the time Donald worked full time with his dad in Brooklyn New York, he was making more than his peers, his first wife placed him on $70,000 per annum when she first met him.

In addition, Donald inspiration came from his brother Fred who died as an alcoholic, meaning, the making of Donald J Trump the 45th President of the United States of America had the root in his father, his late brother Fredrick, and his children, all these would in future become his strengths and weaknesses.

When Donald J Trump eventually moved to Manhattan, his presence was enough to change the landscape of New York Big Apple City, he became the city itself. Trump was not only a real estate guru, he primed himself as a deal make, he ventured into many businesses from the failed Trump University, and Trump Airlines, even Casino and he was a promoter of boxing fights of Mike Tyson and Larry Holmes fights including wrestling. He was not afraid to fail, as he took risks in many ventures, he was a restless entrepreneur.

Trump had his hands in everything that could make money and fame, as a risk taker in 1995, his life and business took a down turn, he went through bankruptcy and business turn around, including his Atlantic City business in New jersey and in all, he emerged victorious and whatever his adversaries had on him, he had answers for them all.

Despite all these, Trump was also a man obsessed with himself, he loved his name, if possible, if he could, he would have changed Manhattan to Trump and he could care less, he plastered his name on all his ventures, those he could not fully owned he franchised and in most cases, those he sold, he kept his name on them.

In 2016 when Bill Orally of Fox News interviewed him few days after he won the presidency, he displayed all the magazines that ever published or made his image the front covers in his study room. He had one other weakness, it was his love for his children, in the same way he was obsessed with his name, and he was with his children.

Trump Tower his residence in Manhattan would in future be the place he interviewed all those who would run the presidency with him in years to come.

(2)

Front Runner

After Trump emerged the overall front runner of the Republican Party in the polls, the larger than life man from New York, Donald Trump took a jab on the front runner of the Democrats, former Secretary of State and former New York briefly, as usual with all his opponents, he branded her with a new name Crooked Hillary and the name became what Hillary was called throughout the election and post-election period.

Senator Hillary Clinton who had expressed her disappointments on Trump's statement on immigration in which Trump described the Mexicans as bunch of rapists and criminals must have crossed the line, everyone thought, had lots of problems to overcome.

Furthermore, Trump said he would build a border wall in the Southern part of America and would even make the country Mexico to pay for it, as ridiculous as it might sound, the statement was assumed to be the worst from any presidential candidates in the modern history of American politics.

How would it be possible to make another country pay for the wall was beyond imagination. Vicente Fox, a former President of Mexico who was even taunted on the news by the Liberal Press to react to the idea of his country paying for the wall in America.

Mr. Vicente Fox said in almost a street language attitude that his country would not pay for the "fucking wall" he jokingly added by the time the wall was ready Mexico too would have completed the ladder to climb the wall back to the United States of America.

Vicente Fox was elected the 55th President of Mexico from 2000 to November 30th, 2006 as he became the first Independent candidate to win the presidency in 71 years, a year after he left office in 2007 he was accused of corruption and enrichment on the ranches he acquired but due to the legal process in his country there had been no update on the charges. Vicente Fox would run again for Mexico Presidency in the year 2020.

Donald Trump's scary words to those who schooled in United States political history were worse than Mike Tyson biting the ears of Evander Holy-flied. All other Republican candidates feared Trump because he was ready to destroy them, or they were even too scared to debate him in his own street language style and what could be closer to his style was the street language between him and Florida State Senator Marco Rubio over the shape of his hand.

All other candidates particularly, the anointed Gov. Jeb Bush of the State of Florida, who was married to a first-generation Hispanic woman was much more confused about the style of Trump, at one stage, Jeb Bush cautioned Donald Trump not to assume he could abuse his way to the White House, and in fact it was what happened, as Trump abused and attacked his way more to Washington DC.

Trump's encounter with Jeb Bush was not only stimulating, it was a witness of the collapse of Bush empire. Trump shrunk the ego of Jeb Bush when he called him *low energy*, when Jeb asked his mother, who had earlier advised him against running for President after his senior brother Bush 43rd to campaign for him, Trump had funny things to say. He was painted as weak and very lacking in almost everything in the same manner as Barack Obama

Unfortunately for Jeb he brought his brother 43rd President George Walker Bush to help with North Carolina primaries, it was the end of everything thing. Trump saw it as an opportunity to kick Jeb more in the ass, he made it look like Jeb was bullied and had to call his mother or brother to defend him, it was childishly presented, and Jeb Bush had no answer for Trump until he dropped out of the race.

The result of the primaries against Jeb and his lectures on the stage by Trump might have finally sealed whatever the Bush had in stock politically in America. It will not be wrong to conclude that Trump retired the Bushes, at one stage, he told Jeb to shut up like a kid with his hand to his lips. He reminded Jeb his horrible four percent in the polls and wondered why Jeb was still on the same stage to debate with him when he had no poll records.

Trump knew and well calculated that Jeb was the biggest fish within the pack of the Republicans in the Primaries, and if he could destroy him others would be like piece of cake, it was rumored that Bush family had asked former Governor Mitt Romney the 2012 nominee not to run again, otherwise, Mitt would have been in the race in the primaries.

In between those personal attacks of Trump on other contestants during the GOP primaries, the Republican Party

Chairman Reince Priebus from Wisconsin had requested Donald J. Trump to tone his words down, but Trump was not backing down.

He was not a man to be controlled, as a business man, he saw his rise in the polls and the enthusiasm of his listeners as a marketing tool and he turned it to all the six P's of marketing strategies, of promotion, price, placement, products, power and politics.

Donald was very quick to let everyone know how rich he was, at least he told everyone who cares to listen, he did not need any donor to run his campaign nor did he have to pay for the free publicity which the American Press gave him every night, his words were news to the both the cable and regular news media. His private Jet branded with his name packed at LaGuardia Airport in Queens New York he did it in styles very unknown in United States of America politics in the last 70 years.

Donald Trump was worth $8.7 Billion unlike the $4.3Billion Forbes source claimed, if he can't use the money and power at his disposal to destroy his adversaries or when would he use it and ugly promotion easily at his disposal if not now? He would be the richest man in modern history to run for the presidency.

However, he moved from being the 92 richest men in America to 244 after his fortune went down after winning the presidency. He will still be first Billionaire to be the President of the United States of America, in modern history.

The opinions and fears of all were that simple, if Trump could participate in the Presidential debates, the first of the nine Republican Party debates was coming up in August, he would destroy not only the party, but the ego and courage of others, he was not afraid to say anything or throw anything at his opponent.

Even if it was in a very dirty form, truthfully, Donald Trump was the heart of how average White Republicans felt about everything including their attitude to immigrants except he was the only one, who could say it out.

In the last 30 years since President Bush signed the Diversity or Lottery Bill sponsored by Democrats, the side effect of it was negative for the Republican Party as increasing immigrants found comfort with the Democrats more than the Republicans, the white technically found their population shrinking to the detriment of the future of its hold on the nation. It became a concern for the White Conservative Americans and everything thing they stood for was under attack, including their values, religion and second amendment on gun ownership.

Donald Trump was not Ross Perot, an independent presidential candidate in 1992 and the Reform Party presidential candidate in 1996, he was not even John McCain the GOP 2008 nominee against Obama who had the opportunity to destroy Barrack Obama but took another route when he was asked to determine if Obama was an American born in Kenya, Trump was not even Mitt Romney the GOP 2012 nominee who was too naive to take the attack to Barack Obama, Donald Trump was his own man free of any control.

Could Donald win the 2016 nomination of his party or destroy the future of Republicans among the Latino's the only group that could propel the GOP back to power?

It was the general opinion from the mainstream Press that Trump as the GOP candidate may never get the Blacks votes, the Party would not get Students votes, it would not get majority of the women's votes, it would not get the votes of the first and second generation of immigrants and due to it stand on same sex marriage, the conservative party, would not get the votes of 10% Americans that were LGBT, the general assumption of the liberal, and that made his Party worried.

Out of the Press, Fox Network news and One America News were his only friends and even Fox, some of the staff were ready to roast him alive, like Kelly Meghan who took the fight straight to him on the stage on his past utterances on women, when Kelly took on Trump in his first of the nine debates in the GOP Primaries, observers knew her days with the Fox network news was over if ever Trump should win the presidency.

Kelly was brutal, and her questions had no feelings for Trump or even the future of the Republican Party, if what she had in mind was to destroy Trump on women he had called names in the past, it was unfairly presented, and Trump went back his Television showdown with Oder Neil as the only woman he had problem with, his recollection brought the funny side of the problem to public and he scaled over the traps of Kelly.

Furthermore, it was also the thinking of average Americans that Donald Trump might have closed the door of the Republican Party to other races like Hispanics, blacks, and Asians with his stands on how China manipulated her currency obviously, he was not expanding the party, to them he was shrinking conservative thinking of the GOP, his mistakes no matter his good intentions may be worse than the 47% Mitt Romney mentioned in his private meeting which was leaked and it cost him the presidency among the economically challenged American in 2012.

As glaring as all the mistakes of the front runner Donald Trump were almost every night events to entertain all and sundries and the stupidity of his party, America's 2016 Presidency was looking good for the Democrats at least on paper, because a President Trump was too scary and he could be another war monger like George Bush, honestly, Hillary Clinton must have smiled to her last Premolars on the journey GOP but the fear of political analysts was if Donald Trump faces Hillary Clinton in the Presidential Debate, he would destroy her with everything including blackmail and some very uncomplimentary statements that may chase her presidency even if she wins, because Trump was a dirty player and aggressive business man with all the three M"s (Money, Material and Men) to throw around.

The consensus was that Donald Trump would not go down easily, he was a fighter and if he must, he would take all the Presidential candidates of his Party down with him, that was the assumptions of his Republican Party in 2016 because he was not a good presidential material for a party like GOP noted for anti-immigration, anti-women's right, students, and medical care for the sick and poor in fact Trump was a nakedness of the Republican Party for its true colors.

Towards, the end of the primaries, Donald Trump was like a rapidly growing stage four Cancer for the Republican Party, and if that part of the body, was not removed quickly, it would kill all the cells of the whole body that was how to assess Trump from New York and the future of his Republican Party.

(3)

Lock her Up

Former Secretary of State Hillary Clinton the Democrat 2016 presidential candidate had paid the price politically for her lies over the use of her personal email for her official duties as Secretary of State over classified document, despite government regulation against the practice and the lies were pulling down her numbers in the polls.

Majority of the Democrats did not trust her anymore, even the liberal press MSBC and her number one fan Mika Brzezinski of Morning Joe talk show looked uncomfortable defending her liar, and like Trump she embellished most her statements, but the records were too glaring to push under the carpet.

The former Secretary of State Hillary Clinton may likely face criminal charges even a possible jail term as FBI had taken over her server to retrieve all the deleted 30,000 emails, her personal assistant Huma Abedin had been requested to submit herself for interrogation.

Abedin was born in Michigan. Her father, Syed Zainap Abedin, was Indian, and her mother, Saleh Mahmood Abedin, was a Pakistani. When she was two years old, her family moved to Jeddah, Saudi Arabia, where she lived until returning to the States for college. Her family had stronger ties to Islamic faith and her mother wrote a book on Sharia.

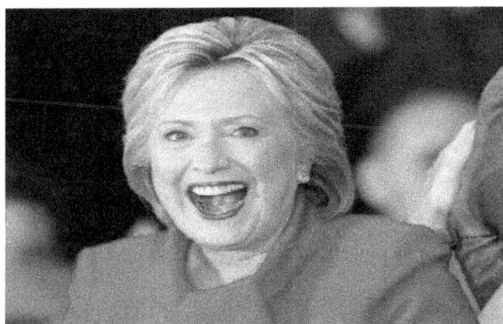

Former US Secretary of State Hillary Clinton

The Clintons had a history of surrogates that went to jail after the prosecutor failed to prove anything like the case in the state of Arkansas James B McDougal in Whitewater investigations died in Fort Worth jail where he was imprisoned and some other suicide cases that could not be proven, whatever it was, the Clintons were never indicted.

What Abedin did with the information on the classified email found on her email to her pervert husband former NY Congressman and her history and connection to Pakistan and Saudi Arabia could be of interest to the FBI in future. It was the fear of in the Democrats inner circle.

Somehow, it was as if she was protected by the Department of Justices under President Obama as the nation watched in disbelief how Huma Abedin got a free pass and it became a concern to the electorate, and every protection Hillary got from Obama presidency made Trump a better candidate.

The ugly part of that new email saga was the same guy who got four-star General David Howell Petraeus indicted, the former CIA boss over similar email stuff to his girlfriend was the same guy on Hillary and how President Obama was going to bend the rules for Hillary Clinton became the subject in the 2016 elections.

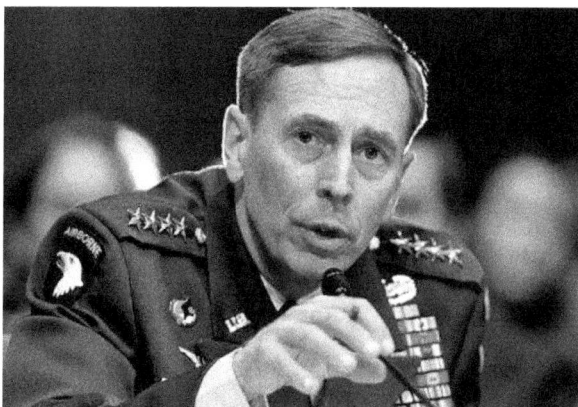

General David Howell Petraeus

(curtesy of AP Photo/Pablo Martinez Monsivais File)

Petraeus was a highly decorated four-star general, who served over 37 years in the United States Army. His last assignment in the Army as commander of the International Security Assistance Force and Commander, U.S. Forces Afghanistan from July 4, 2010, to July 18, 2011.

Gen. Petraeus resigned as Head of the CIA in the wake of revelations that he had carried on an extramarital affair with his biographer Paula Broadwell. The scandal only got weirder with each new detail. Broadwell, who was also married at the time but was anxious that Petraeus' eye was wandering to a Tampa socialite, Jill Kelley, sent Kelley a series of anonymous, threatening emails.

With the help of a dogged (some say obsessed) FBI agent, Kelley got the Bureau on the case, which eventually grew so large it turned to Kelley herself, and to an email exchange — characterized as "flirty" to the AP by a government official — she had with Gen. John Allen.

Petraeus' and Broadwell's use of draft emails in a private Gmail account led to more than a few chuckles that even the nation's top spy couldn't keep his email private.

According to Fox news everything was looking like Whitewater and Hillary Clinton the hope of America first woman President may drop out of the race in the next three weeks and Vice President Joe Biden was warming up in case Hillary drops it will to confirm the prediction of the Oracle, that only a man with a smart mouth like the man from Delaware like Joe Biden can match Mr. TRUMP of New York.

As vulnerable and Hillary was to all the narratives around her it could be right to confirm that Donald Trump was doing just fine, and how he would handle Joe Biden would be something to behold, then Vice President Joe Biden maybe the only guy that can rescue the traumatized Hispanic voters from the claws of Trump of the most comprehensive immigration package ever unleashed in the history of America. It was indeed the fear of all.

However, Joe Biden had two problems in the past, he had faced the problem of plagiarism, and he love to hug women longer than necessary at the time of Hillary crises, he was faced with a fresh bereavement of his son who died of Cancer, psychologically, Joe Biden was not ready for the task ahead.

When the New Yorker Donald Trump was asked if Hillary Clinton would get out of the email saga he said sarcastically, FBI only get involved in criminal cases, not civil, meaning, Hillary Clinton could be a candidate for Federal jail house if that was what Trump was technically telling his viewers that same day in the state of Alabama as usual his crowd were excited and as they shouted, "Lock her Up"

If General Petraeus could be pulled down, why not Hillary Clinton seem to be the opinion of the Republicans?

Hillary Clinton the former Secretary of State and Senator from New York or former first lady was not above the law in America, a country with respect for law and Order, and functioning oversights system from the Congress, if the 1789 Constitution could still be regarded as the guiding light in America.

The bad news was more than what ordinary readers here would want to assume, FBI would retrieve all the information in the deleted thirty thousand emails from the hard-drive, if it contains dirty stuff, on President Clinton himself, his Billion dollar Foundation, his and his wife donors in and out of the country, Monica Lewinski stuff, the Press would love every minute of it, trust the Fox news, trust Mr. Sean Hannity of Fox, and all the Republicans, they were waiting and smiling to their last premolars, and if only they could lay their hands on it, they would devour the Clintons like the Vultures.

However, as the investigations on Hillary Clinton was getting deeper and messy it became obvious that she needed prayers from her fans and those looking up to Hillary as the first female President of America was for the email servers not to end the Clinton's legacy and possible jail terms for many associates, they asked God for miracle, to turn the information in the server to something positive like Jesus turned water to wine, it was the only hope, if not. It was not going to look good in the weeks ahead.

Dr. Ben Carson was not a strange name in the Health Care industry, a neurosurgeon, author, a graduate of University of Michigan Medical School and Director of Pediatrics at John Hopkins Hospital in Maryland from 1984 to 2013 where he retired.

Ben Carson had received more than 60 honorary degrees, dozens of National citations, and had written over 100 Neurosurgical publications in 2008, he received Presidential Medal of Freedom, the highest civilian award in the United States of America.

In 2013 his widely publicized speech of National Prayer Breakfast made him a darling of the conservations and it gave him an idea he could be President.

Senator Marco Rubio, Donald Trump, Dr. Ben Carson

Ahead of United States GOP Presidential Debate slated for September 16th, the stage was now set for Billionaire Donald Trump Vs. Dr. Ben Carson who did not talk much in the last GOP debate but surprisingly, he was rising in the polls, who had even raised almost $20 million, but the question was if Americans can afford a back to back Black President after Obama's presidency? It was doubtful, but it could be possible if the polls were right.

It would be another miracle, honestly, for Ben Carson to win GOP nomination and win the presidency, it was like asking Bill Cosby with his famous Benadryl to fix your wife a drink and thinking it would be just fine. It would be another uphill task because Dr. Carson as President may end up like Justice Clarence of the Supreme Court without any value to the backs in America with his conservative values, since Carson thinks like Clarence.

The stage was set for Mr. Trump to tell Dr. Carson to go back to his clinics or hospitals and talk to the Nurses and Healthcare workers instead of making a couple of jokes and thinking things would be just fine. And if Carson thought he could joke his way to the White House without anything concrete something was wrong somewhere.

Honestly, in the last debate, Carson did not say much, but that was the end of it for him as the CNN organized debate had a rising in poll Carly Fiorina in it, however, Carson would be questioned by the press, he had avoided, so it was with Trump and Carly Fiorina, the debate would be solely among these three non-politicians with nothing for "low energy" Jeb Bush and others that would drop out after the September 16th Debate. It was the way or hope of the nation.

Carly Fiorina was an American business woman whose net worth could around $60 million former Chief Executive officer of HP from 1999 to 2005, the first woman to lead the billion dollar company, HP manufacturer of personal computers and printers, during her time as CEO, the company laid off 30,000 workers in other to save 80,000 jobs later the company grew up to over 150,000 workers, despite the turn around the initial laid off became her problem and she was relieved of the job as CEO, she contested as Senator and lost in the State of California to the incumbent Barbara Boxer a Democrat, she was an adviser to John McCain in 2008 Presidential elections

The Oracle suspected the Kentucky Clerk issue on her refusal to issue Marriage License to the gay would be one of the topics that would be mentioned, in addition to the "Wall of Jericho" of Mr. Trump on the Mexican Borders and the Iranian deal and women rights. In all it would be interesting to see the trio, of

Trump, Carson and Carly Fiorina keeping the established politicians away from the dining table because this is the way it is going to be.

Carly Fiona with Senator Ted Cruz

Again, the Debate ended with thumb up for Trump, he neutralized Carly Fiorina, he even apologized for his misconstrued statement about her look and if Fiorina was thinking or weeping any sentiment as a woman against Trump it did not pull any string, and at the end of the debate It was clearer, both Dr. Ben Carson and Fiorina could not stop Donald Trump on his way to the White House

February 10, 2016 due to poor result in New Hampshire and Iowa, Carly Fiorina suspended her dream and a month after she endorsed Texas Senator Ted Cruz against the front runner Donald Trump who later in April 27th, 2016 selected her as his running mate.

However, Dr. Ben Caron Like Carly Fiorina, a month after Carly left the scene, on March 2, 2016 he too suspended his campaign, he said, he did not see any political part forward and would not attend the next debate in Detroit his home town, in total he his campaign had spent $58 million and most of the money went to the political consultant, fundraising rather than advertisement a week after he suspended his campaign he endorsed Donald J Trump, and both became inseparable.

After Carly and Carson left the stage it became a tougher stage for Donald Trump with Florida Senator Marco Rubio, former Governor of Florida Jeb Bush, Governor John Kasich of Ohio State, and Texas Senator Ted Cruz still were all on his neck. Somehow former Gov. Jeb Bush was the least on the pack of five after a miserable 8% in North Carolina result he too suspended his campaign and subsequently endorsed Texas Senator Ted Cruz.

The next stage was Florida and it would become a first

(4)

Convention

The convention slated for the Quicken Loan Arena in Cleveland Ohio State between July 18th-July 21st, 2016 was full of intrigues, it would be the third time in history Cleveland would host the Republican National Convention and the first since 1936.

The arena would play host to all the 2472 delegates, a simple majority of 1237 delegates was expected to be the winner. Presidential hopeful Donald Trump despite his almost to the actual required delegates, he was not assured of the Republican Party ticket until after the convention, because of many factors from both real and unknown fears and practically his non-acceptance by the establishments.

Trump would have to contend with those who made it to the final and those who drop out and still had their names on the list because they had secured delegates during the primaries, the seven of them had their names on the final date of the voting.

No matter what Trump did his political adversaries increased almost daily like mushrooms, as soon as he crossed one obstacle others propped up and everything was looking as if he was not going to get the ticket on first ballot.

Despite all the rules and backbiting Donald Trump with his Vice President nominee Mike Pence, former Governor of Indiana secured the mandate of the Republican Party.

Donald J Trump (NY) 69.78%

Ted Cruz (TX) 484 (19.58%)

Gov. John Kasich (OH) 125 (5.06%)

Senator Marco Rubio (FL) 123 (4.98%)

Dr. Ben Carson (FL) 7 (0.28%)

Gov. Jeb Bush (FL) 3 (0.12%)

Senator Rand Paul (KY) 2 (0.08%)

Abstention 3 (0.12%)

Donald Trump would have to face another problem with the establishment after winning the nomination of his party, his idea on how the convention and post-convention speech would take became the problems of the newly nominated candidate and the Chairman of the NRC. Priebus

Trump had earlier described the 2012 Convention of GOP and the most boring anyone could imagine, and he wanted his own to be entertaining more like Hollywood game full of celebrities, but most of his assumed friends either declined or were prevented by the party politics. When Trump specifically asked for Don King a former boxing promoter to speak, he was reminded Don King had a history of manslaughter case that would not be too well for the image of the Party.

Former Chicago Bears Coach Mike Ditka also declined to speak, Tim Tebow a listed NFL quarterback did not even appear at the convention, Haskell Lookstein a Jewish Rabbi also declined, Trump never wanted those who spoke against him during the primaries to speak at the convention only Senator Ted Cruz of Texas, and Senator Marco Rubio of Florida graced the Convention even the speech of Ted Cruz was not helpful. Governor John Kasich did not enter the Convention hall despite his state hosted the event, Trump had to tongue lash him.

Donald Trump after introduction by his favorite daughter Ivanka officially became the face of the Republican Party, he accepted the nomination of the Party and the fight would be how to put the Democrat nominee Hillary Clinton out of the line. It would be a bigger task since Democrats had the support of a popular two terms President Barrack Obama, and a favorable system for another first like Barrack Obama, this time, it should be a time for a woman President.

Trump spoke for 75 minutes, the longest speech by any GOP candidates since 1972, he stated America was in crises due to attacks on the Police, and terrorists In America, and he promised law and order and he also promised to limit America participation in global problems and trade deals. He was vicious in his attacks and choice of words on President Obama and Hillary Clinton, he would be the first GOP candidate to reach out to the LGBT.

In all, about 32 million Americans watched live the speech of an unusual candidate that would in future change the country from what it used to be with a movement far right and conservative.

According to CNN/ORC poll Trump did not score more than 41% Gallop poll placed him under 36% and it would be a year the Republicans were not too sure of the outcome of the election, nobody gave him any chance and his speech was regarded as terrible and scaring.

(5)

The Candidate

The GOP Candidate Donald J Trump had to repackage his campaign team following the outbreak of the Russian/Ukraine problem of Paul Manafort in August few weeks after the convention, in August 19th exactly after the convention, Paul Manafort quit Donald Trump Campaign team, a professional political strategist since the era of Gerald Ford.

Trump had no more use for Paul Manafort he had started calling low energy like he did with Jeb Bush in the primaries, and when the Ukraine problem came up, it was time for them to part ways, to his credit, he helped Trump to keep his delegates, he opened like of communication with Washington establishment, and his was responsible for Governor of Indiana Mike Pence and GOP VP nominee, whatever was his shortcomings he delivered on his job like he did with Reagan, Bush 41 and other political assignment he had globally.

Despite his candid support for Trump and his team, Paul never had the same chemistry Trump had with Corey Lewandowski his fired Campaign Manager, behind Paul, Donald Trump was secretly consulting with Corey.

In an article published by New York Time it was clear Paul Manafort and Rick Gates had a lot to hide than Trump could take, eleven weeks to the election Trump was forced to make a decision either to bring back his former Campaign Manager or appoint Kellyanne Conway into the open job of Campaign Manager or upgrade Rick Gates the deputy of Manafort and he went 360 degree, He appointed Kellyanne it was a meeting held in the presence of Steve Bannon, Chairman of Breitbart News   a conservative news outlet also present was late Rogers Ailes, the ousted Fox News Chairman.

The shakeup in Trump campaign team was unexpected, Jared Kushner had expressed concerned over money laundry allegation on Paul Manafort and it could be tied to Trump if he did not drop Paul like hot potato, however, Hillary Clinton was looking for a way to link Trump with Putin and Paul Manafort provided the much-needed link Hillary wanted and mainstream media were looking for it too.

It was a shame on how Paul's past real and unreal could derail the presidential dreams of Donald Trump by a man who was only five months on the job with a campaign which started in 2015, but such it is with politics, Hillary did everything possible to make Trump look like the face of President Putin in America.

If there was any regret of Trump in 2016, it would be the hiring of Paul Manafort because he listened to the establishment and infact to Steve Bannon a close business associate of Paul Manafort, It would be a regret he would have to recalibrate his life with.

(6)

The Winner

What a year and what an interesting last 18 months in United States of America. President elect Donald J Trump was like a soap opera, he took on his listeners every day. He took all the oxygen in the room leaving just very little to all his adversaries gasping for air in the room to survive.

Trump treated them like Jewish adage on reincarnation if you were bad in your previous world, in your second coming, you may end up coming back like a mosquito and who treats mosquitos with kindness?

You could slap to kill or flint it with pesticide to kill the mosquitos and that it was how Trump treated his adversaries they must have done something terrible in the previous world.

Gov Mitt Romney was more of a fool he wanted to reap from where he did not sow and Trump like the master of the game gave Mitt the impression he could get the most important position in America as the face of President he called names.

Trump fed him and not just one time, three times to give Mitt the impression he passed first and second interview in fact he was mocking the man who called him ugly names.

While Hillary Clinton was organizing recount through the back door of Green Party Trump had "Thank you" rallies in the states Hillary was hoping to change the result Trump countered her with a thank you message to remind voters of his promises.

Trump was almost completing his Staff with unquestionable and highly competent Americans that would take his message of "make America great again" to the grassroots and keeping the Speaker Paul Ryan within his elbow while Bill Clinton was ranting.

So far Trump was playing the game with adequate control of the midfield that would open the field for his strikers to score goals. In 28 days, the goals would be coming, like he just forced Boeing Aeronautical company to reduce the cost of Air Force One, so it was, for the man who ran the cheapest election against his opponent.

As a businessman, Trump wanted to reduce cost of government and years of waste so far, so good, he was playing the game and he was still winning.

(7)

Middle East

With the United States of America back on the side of Israel fully from January 20th, 2016 when Donald J Trump becomes US strong President and a good working relationship with Russia begins.

The world better tells those funny Arabs with that funny smiles on their faces to stay away from the back of Israel otherwise, Gaza strip would be taken over fully by Israel.

Five years ago, this writer re-echoed what he said in 1975 that if the Palestinians valued their land let them not attack Israel if they do any captured land becomes Israel territory and all the captured land since 1967 cannot be given back to the war mongering Palestinians for disobeying the 1948 UN resolution on the creation of Israel.

That United Nations vote against Israel was nothing without the might of America and this was the deal, you could quote the Oracle on this. America would trade in the support for Syria rebels like a used car for Israel with Russia as a broker. How?

United States under President Trump would withdraw from any support for any rebel group in Syria and support a Russia backed President Assad to keep his country intact.

In exchange for this deal Russia would close eyes on the occupied territories as alleged by the UN resolution and the Arab world would wake up from dream or nightmare of a recaptured land.

Note this, Jerusalem the City of David would officially be declared the capital of Israel and Arab world could cry if they like. Jerusalem would regain its lost glory.

At home in America, a new sheriff would be in town from January 20th, 2017, the FBI may reopen Hillary Clinton's email and

Clinton Foundation cases to keep her busy and Obama may be asked questions on some of overpriced contracts like the Boeing Aeronautical contract which was renegotiated from $4Billion to $1.5 Billion by yet to be sworn in President elect Trump.

President Obama hanging around in DC would not be in his own interest rather it would be to answer questions and any attempt to make it a race issue may not be fine as the blacks would look back at his achievements if and how it had affected them.

With no appointment of a black Supreme Justice by Obama for them, with 39% of those in Jail that were blacks, with 58% unemployed youths, and crimes and drugs in most black cities and police brutality that happened on his watch particularly in Chicago it was doubtful if any black would follow him.

It was even doubtful if President Obama would get any pressure group against President Trump to prevent conflicts let him go away quietly as it was the practice in America otherwise, he may be making a fool of everything he represents.

(8)

Election Results

Out of 3142 counties (local governments) in America. Hillary Clinton won in a little over 500 counties the rest, for Mr. Donald J Trump of the GOP. Hillary Clinton of DNC big wins in two big cities like New York and LA gave her the popular votes otherwise; she lost bigly like Trump would say in almost 75% of UNITED STATES OF AMERICA counties.

How could a win in New York and LA which were full of liberals and controlled UNITED STATES OF AMERICA Press determine the President of America?

The founding father of America constitution through James Madison in his Virginia report introduced the Electoral College votes to make a winner have the backings of both the small and big cities in the outcome of the election in America on what was called "the fear of intrigue"

How did the 270-electoral college become the winning number? 100 Senators along with all the seats in the Congress fifty percent of it constituted the electoral college votes.

At a time when Mr. Khan the father of a dead American hero from Pakistan who made a keynote address at the Democrat convention asked Donald Trump to read the Constitution he should have asked Hillary Clinton to read the very book that could have helped her to win.

However, Trump read the Constitution as advised by Mr. Khan unlike Hillary who did not particularly the Virginia Report on the fear of intrigue as to the reasons for the inclusion of it in the Constitution.

Trump job approval ratings after his appointment of his White House Staff were now 55% and he had not taken office.

Under Obama the Democrats lost 1003 seats at state and federal level, in the last election 12 Democrats Governors lost for running on Obama record. Hillary lost too on Obama's record. It was unfortunate for President Obama to think he could have won if he had the third chance.

President Obama's record no longer motivated the Americans like it was in 2008 and 2012, the 2016 election was a year for change from Obama policies that ballooned the national debt from $11 trillion to $21 trillion and a complete mess in the middle East. His middle finger last minute action against Israel on UN resolution may not go down well for his legacy.

One good thing about American politics, would be to determine if the mid-term election would determine how effective a Trump administration would be or not but it was the last hope of the Democrats as 18 of the Senators were due for re-election and chances were there for a high performance from Trump may increase GOP current 52 to 62 Senators and that would be enough to amend the porous and weakened areas of the Constitution due to years of liberals in government which may nail the Democrats into a complete political comatose, today the GOP controls more than 32 Governors from 50 states.

Democrats must retool and remove the old hands like Nancy Pelosi from the activity of the Party and must learn to speak like American Party, not like a world controlled party with loyalty to foreign ideologies.

United States of America's flag and Constitution must be enough for them right now, GOP represents the US Flag and US Constitution only and that was the reason GOP won as the Party with loyalty to America and her principle on western civilization.

In the GOP itself there were almost twelves of anti-Trump in the Senate not likely to seek re-election because the signs were that they will likely lose, at the same time it was not likely the Democrats had figured out how to handle President Trump until they won in Alabama Senate seat, which they did with all the Blacks votes and misunderstood white voters over the sexual harassment issue labeled on the GOP candidate Roy Moore.

To win further seats, the Democrats would have to use what they knew better, on policy of blackmail and over blown mainstream media war, on GOP candidates in most of the vacant seats towards the mid-term elections. If it worked against Roy Moore it should work more for the rest of the seats and chances are there, Democrats may grab the Senate from the Republican Party.

To attain this, the DNC would twist and mobilize the press on the policy statement of President Trump and as careless as he could be with his choice of words, it could be the way the DNC could redeem itself towards the Mid-term elections.

(9)

Russian Question

With only three weeks to the end of Obama's administration tomorrow 12/29/16 the President said he would slap punitive actions against Russia over the yet to be released document on hacking of DNC secret on how the Crown Princess of the Party Hillary Clinton cheated on Senator Bernie Sanders with secret emails that made the old man to look like a fool to the electorates and the dirty works of Clinton Foundation.

The above was the sin of Russia, a foreign country that revealed the truth about a candidate in U.S. politics, it would have been better if it was done locally, but a country like Russia with President Putin smiling behind the scene was too much for President Obama.

In a game in which the presidency was expected to be neutral, President Obama campaigned seriously for Hillary, at one stage, they hugged one another with eyes closed it was more than what the "angry White men" (apology to Bill Clinton) and the evangelical Christians could take, to them it was more than politics. Furthermore, Michelle Obama said when GOP go low, DNC would go high, it was like the cell theory in Biology class, the Clinton and Obama cells became one politically as Hillary became the inheritance of Obama's legacy or vice visa.

The Question was how President Obama would enforce the punishment when he was only by the door himself. It takes more than a month to even process the paper work on the pronouncements and he could forget the cooperation of the GOP controlled Senate and House; the GOP House controlled already warming up a resolution to condemn the UN resolution over Israel, he championed.

The only option for President Obama would be executive order which would not be relevant after Jan 20th, 2017 to a vindictive President-Elect Trump. Obviously, President Obama did not study Trump's body language during the GOP primaries whatever you give Trump he would you give back ten times, which was his style and for an outgoing President to make things difficult for Trump was not the end of the movie. It was infact the beginning of it.

Former President Barrack Obama

Whatever, it was, it was a dirty trick of former President Obama on incoming President and If it was a process to make President Trump unpopular, the public were yet to see the rationale behind it. And if it was to make Trump look like a friend of the enemy, that would probably be what the executive order would achieve.

It was the practice in US politics to set up traps for any incoming administration to battle with and it was how the incoming President handles the problems that would make his Party win or lose the mid-term elections. It was always the last ugly fight from any outgoing President from a Party which lost the general elections, Obama would not know what he was doing.

President Clinton did the same ugly stuffs for incoming President George Bush after his Vice President Al Gore lost in a controversial election in 2000 and the carelessness of President Bush for not reading traps set by Bill Clinton probably led to 9/11 attack and Bill Clinton was so petty with it that the keyboards in the White House with B characters on them were removed.

However, George Bush was a decent man he never made things difficult for Obama in 2008, he distanced himself from any topic that would have made him to attack the President both in the private and public meaning, Democrats did not know how to handle defeat was the keyword here. They behaved like the wailers and unfortunately for them Donald Trump was not like President George Bush, he had no temperament to be nice to anyone who gave him problem, from his record he would give it back to Obama and Hillary Clinton just as the years continued.

(10)

Russia Again!!

Americans saw how and why both President Obama and Prime Minister Netanyahu threw jabs at themselves openly to the happiness of the enemies of the two nations.

Israel was almost like the unmentioned 51st state of the United States of America, far away like Hawaii the 50th state. It harbors the best brain of America inventors from Cell Phone to Space ventures, the cooperation between the two nations including the cover up democracy in the middle East was not what anyone with the love for Islam based on the principle of Ottoman Empire was happy with.

Let us restore the old glory of our people had always been in the mind of everyone in the middle East if you were a Muslim you would want the Ottoman and Persians back. It was the reason the Muslim brotherhood was founded in 1928 founded in Egypt as a transnational Sunni Islamist Organization by Islamic school teacher Hassan al-Banna, the goal was to instill the Quran and Sunnah as the Sole reference point for all in ordering the life of the Muslims family, individual, community and state, for many years the organization was financed by Saudi Arabia

If you were Jewish, King David might, and glory would be your dream, to the old Jerusalem for its glory and restoration of the great Temple built by his son King Solomon. With the way the Quran wrapped itself in most of the prophets and Kings of the Jews, very doubtful if Islam as a religion that could exist without the history of the Jews and their Kings and prophets, it was also a religion that could not be sanctified without the stories in the

Christian Bible and Jewish Torah and somehow, the Quranic version of the stories both in Torah and Bible did not totally support what Quran mentioned about Jewish history.

Each day the believers in Quran see the Jews differently, it was like being looked at by a person who could puncture your story or religion with their own facts. I have in the past questioned what would the Quran look like if it did not contain the stories in Torah and Bible?

I can't see it.

While the Muslims relied on the stories of Angel Gabriel to Prophet Mohamed as the story of God (Allah) and Jews unfortunately for the Muslims, the Bible and Torah recorded their own history with facts and figures and the Angel Gabriel in the Bible did not tell the same stories about God in the same way the Mohamed version of the Angel Gabriel did.

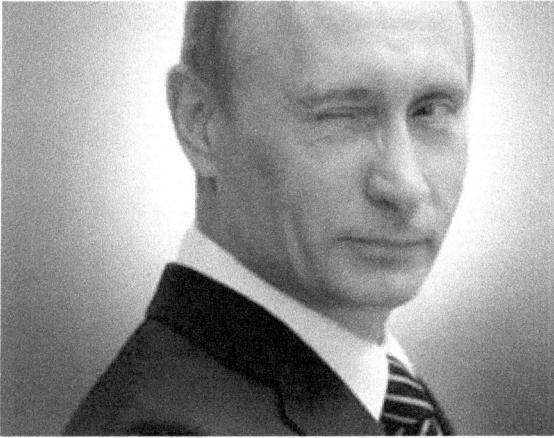

President Vladimir Putin of Russia

The above was the reason why Israel must never be freed, and her freedom would be a revelation of questions the Muslim world would always be uncomfortable with including their spiritual places.

By the time the British returned the Jews back to their Biblical home, the Muslims world became uncomfortable because Israel got her freedom from everyone and spiritual freedom would give them the right to tell the world their stories not what any Angel Gabriel told anyone or any other religion.

The killings of the Jews did not start today, it was the same killings that forced the British to move for the freedom and creation of the State of Israel in 1948 through the United Nations.

The last paragraph of part six took a cursory look at the implications of President Obama's last-minute fight against Israel on 1967 border and how would President Trump handle it.

Somehow, as we were about to find a cleaner for that mess, between Obama and Netanyahu, the issue of Russia came in and Trump first 100 days was looking with more work that may remove his hairs.

(12)

Last Days

18 days more to the new administration, Obama struggled to do his eight years jobs in 20 days with his executive orders, it could just be like how Trump described Jeb Bush who suddenly found his energies in the last minutes of his failing GOP primaries.

Somehow, electorates were wondering why and what happened to President Obama's energies In the last eight years when Police brutality was going on and killing the blacks or when the Chinese hacked the Federal Workers Personnel records and he did nothing?

It could be the reason Puff Daddy said, "we have been shortchanged with Black President stuff".

With Obama's last-minute efforts to create road blocks for the newly elected President with Israel and Russia it was doubtful if another black man may be trusted as President of America for a long time.

To conclude the series with the following words on President Obama, he made history as the first black President unfortunately, he did not fulfill the dreams of Martin Luther king Jr. or what was the purpose of history he made, if it cannot open the doors for other black politicians to get to the same level like him? Obama like Obasanjo closed door and it would take a long time to open.

As an African American of Africa decent, one could see the DNA of a former President in Africa in President Barack Hussein Obama who after second term was looking for third term which was not in the Constitution and when he failed, he made sure his successor had problems, that would be how to assess Obama and his third term dream through Hillary Clinton and when he failed, the African in him came out with his last-minute executive orders.

(13)

The Kennedy Legacy

President Obama owed the Clintons a lot of gratitude on many issues Barack Obama never had any clear-cut agenda of his own before he ran for Office of President in 2008

When I visited President Clinton's Library in Little Rock and his birthplace in Hope Arkansas a year after Obama won the Presidency, I discovered everything Obama was doing was modeled after all the reports in the Clinton's Library.

Obama presidency was more of the third term of President Bill Clinton infact most of the takeoff staffs of Obama were mostly from Clinton previous administration. Everything was taken from the Library if you doubt this post take a visit to President Clinton's Library. The Secretary of State Job given to Hillary Clinton in 2008 was not enough; the Clintons needed the Presidency more than Obama. If Bill had his way, Al Gore would have succeeded him in 2000 until President Bush came from nowhere to win.

The dream of Obamacare was infact Hillary care in 1993, the foundation of Obama care could not honestly be taken as that of Barack, though it could have his signature it was more like the Biblical hands of Esau and voice of Jacob Obamacare was indeed Hillary care, it was what and how she reminded the voters,

However, the foundation of all US Healthcare system from Obama to Hillary including Medicare and Medicaid belongs to Late Senator Kennedy who introduced Wheelchair into all Hospitals and Nursing Homes in America.

Truthfully, both Obama, and Hillary were disciples of Senator Kennedy of Massachusetts on Health care laws, when the Lion of the Senate Kennedy came out of the Hospital to vote in support of the Bill, it was like a dream fulfilled.

---

(14)

Foreign Policy

From January 20th, 2017 a President Trump would make peace with President Putin of Russia in writing and both would work out their areas of differences and Trump would be the guest of Putin Russia in Moscow same with Putin in the White House it would be the end of cold war between the two nations. Note the following as they would be unfolding as predicted by this writer known as the Oracle.

1. United States of America would dump the Rebels in Syria for President Assad to fix his country.

2. US and Russia would revisit the last UN resolution on Israel on 1967 border to reflect progress made in the last 40 years.

3. NATO would either admit Russia into its fold or wind down, as funds would be cut off which would be part of the deal, in exchange, ISIL may be Nukes out of existence like a drop of Hiroshima or Gen Pershing policy and Turkey may be kicked out of NATO if it is unable to keep its house in order.

4. North Korea would be handled by both Russia and US through tougher actions.

4A. on trade with China. A China without US market would collapse pushing almost 1.3 Billion Chinese into political unrest, most likely 60 percent of US companies in China would relocate back home under a very conducive economics and political policies of President Trump.

5. Saudi Arabia must fix her problems with Iran over Sunni and Shiite to solve the radical Islamist terrorists within the two groups or be Nukes out existence or the application of General Pershing pig policy on them.

6. US would officially declare Jerusalem the Capital of Israel and all the Biblical Holy places back to Israel. US Embassy may move to Jerusalem from Tel Aviv.

7. More Islamic Organizations in the Middle East like Muslim Brotherhood may be declared terrorist organizations, if they fail to reform as US intelligence would listen to their hate messages to determine how their nation would be treated. Adoption of General Pershing principle on how the terrorist would be treated.

8. Only two areas would be of Interest to President Trump in Africa. How the Christians were treated in Nigeria, a revisit of 1914 Amalgamation and Biafra issues. Also, Egypt in cooperation with President Sisi US would end Muslim Brotherhood terrorist actions in the North Africa.

9. Extreme vetting of Muslims from all nations would be pursued, to enter United States of America you would be asked to take a vow against that funny Sharia law not to act or dream of it in America or you would be deported, and your country would pay for deportation cost.

10. Immigrants to America would sign a paper to agree they were coming into a nation with Western Civilization and any primitive thinking should be dropped at the border. This policy was not new it is the same in most Islamic nations.

11. Immigrants to America would raise their hands to uphold the laws of America, not the thinking of foreign religion. Only friends would enter America not enemies under President Trump meaning those ready to adopt America ways of life.

12. Since it costs money to deport a criminal or illegal immigrant, your country of origin would pay the cost in a bilateral agreement with all nations doing business with America meaning, your country would be involved before you could ask U.S. Embassy for Visa like collateral for visa loan in case you have to be deported. Something like that.

13. To obtain a US Visa, you would take online class on the values and history of America to understand why certain actions and values became part of American culture to prevent cultural shock that could radicalize any immigrant.

14. Guantanamo bay detention camp in Cuba would remain active and Russia would be encouraged to reopen the detention camps in Russia for enemy's exchange program.

15. Cuba must reform or the deal with President Obama would be off the table.

16. Iranian deal is off the table on the first month of President Trump and it would face very hostile US policies if the nation is still thinking of NUKES.

17. US would work with Russia and Britain on a new Oil Cartel to send OPEC parking in addition to the keystone pine line from Canada to make foreign oil unnecessary in North America. It would be a tough time for the enemies of America under President Donald J Trump.

(15)

Anticipated Dream

Former US President Barack Obama said he could have won the last Presidential elections against the eventual winner President Trump if there was a provision for it in the Constitution, he said he knew how to articulate his points better than Hillary Clinton.

The above statement was taken beyond the context of its ordinary meaning, as a third term ambition by almost Republicans nonetheless, it was a sign of frustration on the part of President Obama.

It would necessary to ask if Obama was right on that assumption or not? Taking cognizance of his post presidency behavior to make in-coming administration of President Trump uncomfortable.

President Obama may be right as he currently led the post White House political discussion from behind the scene like he did in office which ended in political disaster for his party that lost everything he met in 2008 like Clinton and Bush, the House, the Senate and a Liberal Supreme court. Obama lost them all in 2016 to the GOP.

Surprisingly, or intentionally, for his daughter's education or so, President Obama took a residency in Washington DC instead of Chicago or Hawaii after he left office about two miles away from the White House, and no President in United States modern history ever shared Washington DC, the Capital of America and center of all world events with a sitting President, not even after a very ugly election.

That election result in 2016 gave victory to the other side despite the energies President Obama exacted into the campaign including name calling and mocking the eventual winner Donald J Trump, who never ran for any office in his life not even as a council member in Manhattan New York.

Apart from building Hotels, Apartments, Golf courses all over the world and other retail business the only government experience of Donald was donations to all politicians Democrats, Republicans and Independents that could make his business flourish.

Trump's Television shows made him a tough guy and a risk taker and when the Obama's birth certificate became the issue that threatened the legitimacy of Obama's right to US number one job Trump was in the forefront of it. He saw in it an opening that made him the darling of the Republican Party

Donald Trump involvement was deeper than ordinary, he placed a five million dollar bet on it if Obama could provide the long hand-written birth certificate and no one could tell what could have happened if Obama was unable to meet the demand.

Somehow, President Obama did and even at a White House Correspondent dinner he made fun of Trump. It was at that point those closer to the man born in Queens to Fred Trump, the Brooklyn Real Estate Developer made up his mind to take a shot at the number one position of the land.

2012 was the year Trump wanted to do it, but he was prevailed upon to shift his ambition for Gov Mitt Romney, he later supported in cash and kind. When Mitt Romney lost to Obama in 2012 Trump was bitter and made up his mind to use all available strategies to campaign in 2016

The road was tougher than it was expected for Trump and probably tougher than 2012 he had wanted to run. 2016 elections were indeed a gang up of all the three political machines and establishment including the mainstream media, the Bush and Clinton machines in America politics since Ronald Reagan in the eighties and Obama political machines in the White House.

In the same way, Trump, had notified the nation for decades that China and Mexico may be responsible for US economy problem and increase in National debts due to NAFTA and TPP, his messages on trade were not new. His trade businesses worldwide gave him a better view of where the problem that increased the national debt by more than a trillion was.

(16)

The role of Russian, China and Mexico

What was even the job of any ambassador if not to watch out for his country's interest in a foreign land technically, an ambassador is nothing but a spy for his country in a foreign nation, that will a very honest and simple way to define it

All the spies in any country of post were there at the pleasure of the ambassador such a nation, he cannot claim ignorance of any of their actions.

China and Mexico because of the favorable situations with President Obama's administration took side with Democrats and Russia because of Obama's failures in Syria and Ukraine took side with Republicans in the last election. And what could have happened if Hillary Clinton had won the 2016 elections?

Would the country be faced with China and Mexico collusion? With massive support from the Liberal press, it could be doubtful.

Despite the friendliness of Kislyak US Ambassador to all political institutions in Washington since 2008, President Obama never trusted President Putin after the former KGB made him to look little with policy of leading from behind.

How could anyone without Russian experience or connection deal with Russia?

Russia Ambassador Kislyak

It became the issue of the day or it would amount to vetting away all candidates and nobody in DC would be qualified for any job because Ambassador Kislyak had been a friend to all of them since President Obama pressed the reset button through Hillary Clinton in 2009.

China and Mexico became terrified about the future of their trade which made US weaker and helpless and the new direction of Trump may reverse the ugly mess of the past.

If the unfavorable $800 Billion trade imbalance was the major problem with China, it would be difficult to manage the effect of it on the 1.4 Billion population without the purchasing power to buy made in China products, because of that, export trade became the Chinese major problem.

Mexico was worried beyond trade of just $70 Billion annually, it was more on the immigration and the role of LA-RASA on the southern states historical link to Mexico and what to do with drugs from Latin America particularly Columbia in which Mexico was the hub for all drugs to the United States of America.

If President Trump was going to be a threat with the border wall and citizenship procedures that may reduce the Caucasians to minority in the next 25 years, then Mexico must be in trouble, including chain migration associated with Green Card system. Countries like Haiti, Ecuador, and Venezuela with economic and natural problems in the past had enjoyed immigration waiver

However, the loss of 2016 presidential elections were a big blow to the DNC agenda. It prevented the amendment of the 1789 Constitution to reflect the new America dreams base on values comfortable to foreign ideologies. It prevented nomination of Liberal Supreme Court judges that could have made it possible to shift the Constitution to what probably would have destroyed the GOP White House dream for 16 years.

Towards the end the election, former President Bush lamented that he may be the last GOP President because everything and every poll did not give Trump a chance to win.

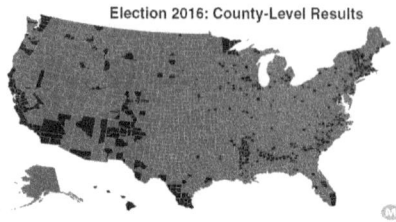

Election 2016: County-Level Results

2016 Electoral College Counties map

However, Donald Trump won the presidency through the fear of intrigue which James Madison the 5.4 ft. tall inserted into the US Constitution with the Virginia proposal to prevent states like Texas, New York and California from hijacking the presidency because of population.

In 1789, James Madison had envisaged the problem of smaller states in midst of bigger states like New York, California, Texas and Florida, it was the basis for the insertion of the electoral college into the 1789 Constitution, under the fear of intrigue, by the time the result of the 2016 Presidential result was released.

The fear of Madison could be confirmed, out of the 3260 counties in the country Hillary Clinton with over three million popular votes could only make it in 525 Counties, and yet Donald John Trump excelled in more than 2700 counties meaning if popular votes was used Hillary Clinton with 15 percent of the counties won would have been US President which was not evenly spread across the nation.

(17)

Post-election tricks of President Obama

President Obama and Hillary Clinton

When you burn your bridges how would you make a comeback? Or in one African adage among the Yoruba after they noticed the behavior of the colonial masters before they left. They made a mess of the room for the incoming leadership to clean up.

President Obama over campaigned for Hillary Clinton against eventual winner President Trump. He took it too personal and it was doubtful if both could find peaceful relationship after the result. It would not be wrong to say President Obama poisoned the water not only for himself, he did it for all African Americans to see the winner Donald Trump as the enemies of what he failed to do for them as the first Black President.

Did Obama live the dreams of Martin Luther king Jr.? Probably not. If yes, maybe in future, but very difficult to pinpoint.

The only African American in the Supreme court was not an appointee of Democrats, Bush 41 appointed him. Maybe if Obama had given African Americans another Supreme Court Justice his legacy would have been solid. He did not even think of it. His home state and City in Chicago recorded the highest crimes in the country at end of his presidency Obama like the previous Democrat President Bill Clinton did not return home unlike the two Republican Presidents from Texas.

The last Bush Presidents, Bush 41st and Bush 43rd both returned to the warming arms of Texans, the same could not be said of the last two Democrats presidents, Bill Clinton did not return to Arkansas, he claimed his stay in New York was a demonstration of his love for the African American community, the reason given was nothing but a bullshit, it was to pave way for his wife to run for President in future which was not possible in Arkansas, a deep red state.

Few months after Hillary Clinton lost election, the Clinton property in Chappaqua New York got raised down by fire and it will not be long before the Clinton will move to another State.

(18)

African Policy of Obama

In the same way, the African Americans felt shortchanged with President Obama's leadership, those in Africa could not point to anything concrete he did for the continent despite the DNA claim they had with Barack Obama Senior.

President Bill Clinton despite his shortcomings created AGOA to help African business to ship products to US while President Bush did more for African than any President in American history but how could Obama, a son of a Kenyan father shortchanged the continent more than his predecessors?

Former Lt. Governor, Michael Steel a former RNC Chairman analyzed the achievement of President George Bush for Africa, he placed Bush way up ahead of Obama and Clinton.

Boko Haram an affiliate of ISIS in NE of Nigeria

In Africa, Nigeria suffered more than any of the 54 countries in the continent because of the law against LGBT. 14 years' jail term for any gay or lesbian activity as punishment was a law signed by President Jonathan despite the pressure from United States of America.

Former President Goodluck Jonathan had informed President Obama that the Gay right he was promoting to Africa was alien to the culture and tradition of Africans after the National Assembly in Nigeria sent a Bill to his office for his signature. The Bill made homosexual or gay rights illegal with a stiffed penalty of 14 years imprisonment, and President Obama request the Nigerian President not to sign the bill into law, and if he if he did there would be consequences from the bilateral relationship with the United States under his leadership and would not be kind to Nigeria which depended on a mono product oil market to sustain the 180 million population.

However, President Jonathan faced with a very hostile National Assembly at home, signed the Bill, the line was drawn between the two countries.

More also, Kenya the home country of Obama Senior rejected the Gay rights, it became a show down between United States of America and Nigeria. It was more like a replica of 1976 political disagreement between President Gerald Ford of the United States of America and General Muritala Mohammed Head of State of Nigeria on who to support over Angola issue.

General Muritala Mohamed ordered the United States Ambassador out of his office at Dodan Barracks then in Lagos and somehow, Nigeria backed Augustinho Neto group who won the election against Savinbi and it was not pretty for the United States ego in Africa, on February 13th, 1976, General Muritala Mohamed was killed in military Coup de-tat, his death was rumored to have the hands of US CIA.

In a reaction to the new law against the Gay rights signed by President Jonathan of Nigeria, President Obama stopped the only means of economic survival of Nigeria, the purchase of the crude oil market since 1968 and Nigeria which never had any plan B for its economy took a down turn.

Secondly, Boko Haram was not classified as a terrorist organization despite the plea from a helpless President Jonathan without military backgrounds and instead President Obama administration held secret meetings with Northern Governors in Nigeria and in Washington DC as if he had a different agenda to divide the country.

Selective meetings with Northern Governors in diversified nation with more than 225 languages and barrier based on religion and tribal sentiments, the meeting excluded the Governors from the South of Nigeria most from the Christian base of the country and it gave the impression Obama had a sinister plan against the largest black African nation with over 180 million population.

On March 14th, 2014, Ambassador Susan Rice met with the Governors from the North of Nigeria in Washington DC, the agenda was to discuss violence and insurgence movement in that part of the country, at least that was the impression they gave the public from a secret meeting, however, it was a meeting held to undermine the authority of President Jonathan, after the similar one held in Nigeria by Vice President Joe Biden.

The most disappointing was the issue of Ebola Virus which President Obama neglected Africa, and Nigeria through her medical team provided the solution to the virus that killed thousands in West Africa.

Only South Sudan, Kenya and Liberia received grants from America, President Obama cut off military grants to Egypt after a radical Islamic government of the Muslim brotherhood was kicked out to prevent Egypt from going to war with Israel over the support of then President Morsi support for the Palestinian hardliners.

Unknown to most political analysts President Obama sold the Americans a dummy on Russia to take the heat off his administration after office and instead of GOP discussing China and Mexico over the trade imbalances, they were busy chasing Russia involvement in election all Ambassadors of every country with interest in America participated.

Unfortunately, Democrats supported China and Mexico input while Republican leaned more towards the Russian. Democrats lost the election with the electoral college in the constitution while the Democrats got more votes outside the requirements of the Constitution thereby lost the election.

To regroup and divert attention from his failed policies of leading from behind former President Obama made a big issue of Russia to keep the Republicans in the three arms of government busy while China and Mexico that were the target of Trump's campaign would find time to regroup.

China through the United States based IMF got the clearance to have her Yuan compete with US Dollars, China is also get all the time to copy US technology from any US companies planning to move out of China back to US.

The group of five, China, Russia, Brazil, India and South Africa formed a cartel against United States dollars, unfortunately, President Obama never considered it a threat as China economic strength continue to grow in Asia, Africa and into South America and US influence shrinking, it was not long before China took the world number one economic spot from America.

(19)

The swam

What a year and what an interesting last 18 months in United States of America presidential run. The President elect Donald J Trump was like a soap opera, he takes you on every day. He took all the oxygen in the room leaving just very little to all his adversaries gasping for air in the room to survive.

Trump treated them like Jewish adage on reincarnation if you were bad in your previous world, in your second coming, you may end up coming back like a mosquito and who treats mosquitos with kindness?

You could slap to kill or flint pesticide to kill the mosquitos and that it is how Trump treats his adversaries from the look of thing they must have done something terrible in the previous world if the Jewish revelation of re-incarnation was anything to go by.

Gov. Mitt Romney was a fool to even think he wanted to reap from where he did not sow was the opinion of those who worked for Trump, former Governor of Arkansas, Mike Huckabee and former New York Mayor Rudi Giuliani all called him names and Trump like the master of the game gave Mitt the impression he could get the most important position in America as the face of President he called names.

Donald Trump fed him and not just one time, three times to give Mitt Romney the impression he passed first and second interview while in fact he was mocked the man who called him ugly names in the primaries.

While Hillary Clinton was organizing recount through the back door of Green Party, President elect Donald J Trump had several "Thank you" rallies in the states Hillary was hoping to change the result, however, Donald Trump countered her with a thank you message to remind voters of his promises.

Within 20 days of his post-election result, Donald Trump almost completed his Staff with unquestionable, tested and highly competent Americans that would take his message of "make America great again" to the grassroots and keeping the Speaker Paul Ryan within his elbow, while Hillary Clinton was ranting.

If the United States politics was a game of soccer, one would be right to say that Trump played the game with adequate control of the midfield, that would open the field for his strikers to score goals.

In 28 days, the goals would be coming, like he just forced Boeing Aeronautical Company to reduce the cost of Air Force One, so it was and even a big plus for the man who ran the cheapest election against his opponent.

As a businessman, Trump wanted to reduce cost of running government in Washington DC and years of waste so far, so good, he played the game and he appeared to be winning, when he called

Washington swamp everyone knew what he had in mind, to cut and minimize wastes.

(20)

Problems

With the United States of America back on the side of Israel fully from January 20th next year when Donald J Trump becomes US strong 45th President and a good working relationship with Russia will start hopefully.

The world better tells those funny Arabs with that funny smiles on their faces to stay away from the back of Israel otherwise, the Oracle says the Gaza strip would be taken over fully by Israel.

Five years ago, this writer re-echoed what he said in 1975 that if the Palestinians valued their land, let them not attack Israel if they do, any captured land becomes Israeli territory and all the captured land since 1967 cannot be given back to the war mongering Palestinians for disobeying the 1948 UN resolution on the creation of Israel.

As usual, the United Nation's vote against Israel will be nothing without the might of America and this was the deal, America may trade in the support for Syria rebels like a used car for Israel with Russia as a broker.

How?

United States of America under President Trump may even withdraw from any support for any rebel group in Syria and support a Russia backed President Assad to keep his country intact.

In exchange for this deal, Russia would close eyes on the occupied territories as alleged by the UN resolution and hopefully the Arab world would wake up from dream or nightmare of a recaptured land.

Note, Jerusalem the City of David will likely to be declared the capital of Israel in future or when and if a President Trump would make it to Israel and Arab world would cry if they like and very likely the United States of America would regain its lost glory a last-minute plan could change the possibility of Jerusalem being the recognized Capital of Israel from Tel Aviv.

Ten months in office, President Trump did not sign the waiver on postponement of the Capital from Tel Aviv to Jerusalem, he infact declared the City of David the Capital of Israel, December 6th, 2017 based on Jerusalem Act of 1995 signed by President Clinton.

At home in America a new sheriff would be in town from January 20th, 2017, new FBI Director may reopen Hillary Clinton's email and Clinton Foundation cases to keep her busy and the former President Barrack Hussein Obama may be asked questions on some of overpriced contracts like the Boeing Aeronautical contract which was renegotiated from $4Billion to $1.5 Billion by yet to be sworn in President elect Trump.

President Obama hanging around in DC would not be in his own interest rather it would be to answer questions and any attempt to make it a race issue may not be fine as the blacks would look back at his achievements if and how it had affected them.

With no appointment of a black Supreme Justice by Obama for them, with 39% of those in Jail that were blacks, with 58% unemployed youths, and crimes and drugs in most black cities and police brutality that happened on his watch particularly in Chicago it was doubtful if any black would follow him.

It was even doubtful if President Obama would get any pressure group against President Trump to prevent conflicts let him go away quietly as it was the practice in America otherwise he may be making a fool of everything he represents.

As the pressure was mounting from the far left the Inspector General in both FBI and Department of Justice reopen cases against Clinton Foundation, Uranium sales deal to Russian and Dossier used by FBI to spy on Candidate Trump, it recorded its first casualty when an associate of Clinton Lambert was indicted, and many heads would still role.

(21)

Last days of Obama

With only three weeks to the end of Obama's administration tomorrow December 29th, 2016 the President said he would slap punitive actions against Russia over the yet to be released document on hacking of DNC secret on how the Crown Princess of the Party cheated on Senator Bernie Sanders with secret emails that made the old man to look like a fool to the electorates and the dirty works of Clinton Foundation.

The above was the sin of Russia, a foreign country which revealed the truth about a candidate in U.S. politics, it would have been better if it was done locally by the press but a country like

Russia with Putin smiling behind the scene was too much for President Obama.

In a game in which the presidency was expected to be neutral, President Obama campaigned seriously for Hillary, at one stage they hugged one another with eyes closed it was more than what the "angry White men" (apology to Bill Clinton) and more than the evangelical Christians could take, to them, it was more than politics.

Michelle Obama said when GOP go low, DNC would go high, it was like the cell theory in a Biology class, the Clinton and Obama cells became one politically as Hillary became the inheritance of Obama's legacy.

The Question was how President Obama would enforce the punishment when he was only by the door himself. It takes more than a month to even process the paper work on the pronouncements and he could forget the cooperation of the GOP controlled Senate and House, the GOP House controlled already warming up a resolution to condemn the UN resolution over Israel.

The only option for President Obama would be executive order, which would not be relevant after Jan 20th, 2017 to a vindictive Trump. Obviously, President Obama did not study Trump's body language during the GOP primaries whatever you give Trump he would you give back ten times, that was his style and for an outgoing President to make things difficult for Trump was not the end of the movie.

If it was a process to make President Trump unpopular the Oracle was yet to see the rationale behind it. And if it was to make Trump look like a friend of the enemy that would probably be what the executive order would achieve.

It was the practice in US politics to set up traps for any incoming administration to battle with and it was how the incoming President handles the problems that would make his Party win or lose the midterm elections. It was always the last ugly fight from any outgoing President from a Party which lost the general elections.

President Clinton did the same ugly stuffs for incoming President George Bush after his Vice President Al Gore lost in a controversial election in 2000 and the carelessness of President Bush in reading traps set by Bill Clinton probably led to 9/11 attack and Bill Clinton was so petty with it that the keyboards in the White House with B characters on them were removed.

However, George Bush was a decent man, he never made things difficult for Obama in 2008 and he distanced himself from any topic that would have made him to attack the President both in the private and public.

Meaning Democrats, particularly, Hillary and Obama did know how to handle defeat was the keyword here, they behaved like the wailers and unfortunately for them, Donald Trump was not like President George Bush, he had no temperament to be nice to anyone who gave him problems from his record, he would give it back to Obama and Hillary Clinton.

(22)

Change

In the United States of America, when they want a change, no matter the approval ratings of a sitting President they would move on. Before the November 8th, 2016 elections, unemployment was less than 5% and Obama's job approval ratings at 55% yet he could not help Secretary Hillary Clinton to succeed or protect his legacy.

Why?

Despite the achievements of his administration, some functional American electorates looked at his failures more than his successes, to them, the death of Osama bin Laden by the Navy Seal was no longer what could make them to follow him again. $21 trillion dollars national debt was too, much to comprehend and his boyish looking was gone and what else could he offer after two terms?

Nothing.

To them, Hillary Clinton did not appear like apostle of change, she had her history dated to her days as first lady in the state of Arkansas and she confirmed in one of the interviews that it was harder running as agent of change with Obama's eight years record hanging around.

At the same time, what President Obama was asking Americans to do to vote for Hillary Clinton could be likened to what President Reagan did for George H Bush the 41st President in the eighties.

However, Bush George had no baggage like Hillary Clinton, and Gov. Mike Huckabee who succeeded Bill Clinton in the state of Arkansas as a Governor said Secretary Hillary Clinton had more baggage than Delta Airlines right from her days as First lady in the state of Arkansas to the office of Secretary of State.

In the nineties, President Bush had won the Desert storm war against Saddam Hussein over Kuwait and he was so confident like President Obama of 2016 at the Presidential debate he was looking at his watch and felt somehow as if the electorates ought to just rubber stamp him for second term, President George Bush was wrong.

President H Bush looked with contempt then Bill Clinton, a Governor from one of the poorest states in America. What was Arkansas State without watermelon and Wal-Mart in 1992?

Nothing, just nothing.

The scandals of women around the neck of a very handsome Bill Clinton particularly that of Paula Jones who openly accused Bill of indecent exposure of his manhood to her in the hotel.

Bill Clinton won, and Bush 41 lost with grace, in 1992 Presidential elections, as painful as it was, Bush Senior took his defeat with respect for the electorates decision, his action was very close to what Vice President Richard Nixon did in 1960 elections when the elections was massively rigged in favor of then Senator JF Kennedy in the State of Illinois, particularly, from Chicago, despite all reasonable evidences, Vice President Nixon moved on.

In 1992, a defeated President George H Bush thanked the people and offered to help a newly elected Bill Clinton even in his prayers. He was a decent man.

However, by 2000 elections, with scandals around a popular Bill Clinton after his two terms in office, his Vice President Al Gore thought he could do it alone. He distanced himself away from a popular Clinton with over 67% approval ratings, it was the worst political miscalculation of the century.

The result was not only heartbreaking, it was a setback for the legacy of Bill Clinton who was shooting for a debt free country which he had inherited $8trillion from former President George H Bush, by the end of his presidency, he had reduced the debt by $3trillion, it was the plan then that with his Vice President Al Gore in the White House and a robust economy, United States of

America was going to be debt free like the era of President Andrew Jackson in 1835.

To the surprise of the political pundits, Al Gore lost even his home state of Tennessee and Arkansas that of Bill Clinton and sheepishly banking on Florida to win, it never happened, he lost, even though it was assumed to have been rigged in favor of George Bush, what about his home state and that of his boss Bill Clinton?

The above was the lesson Hillary Clinton thought she could do without in 2016 elections not to undertake the same hopeless journey as Vice President Al Gore who failed to embrace Bill Clinton with his scandals.

Hillary Clinton in her own case not only embraced President Obama policies, she hugged him openly, it was closer to what the black Actor Cody did in box office movie "Jerry McGuire" on how he made Tom Cruise to show shout "Show me the money" and " I love Black people"

Hillary Clinton a married woman, hugged President Obama openly with her eyes closed and Obama did not open his own either both had baggage than the functional electorates could stomach, functional electorates in the battleground states of PA, FL, NC and others saw how choleric both were and by their wisdom or otherwise voted against her or Obama tired policies.

With only 18 days more to the new administration, Obama struggled to do his eight years jobs in 18 days with his executive orders; it could just be like how Trump described Jeb Bush who found his energies in the last minutes of his failing GOP primaries.

It was how Obama found his energy, and electorates were wondering why and what happened to President Obama's energies in the last eight years when Police brutality was going on and killing the blacks or when the Chinese hacked the Federal Workers Personnel records and he did nothing?

It could be the reason Sean Combs said the African Americans were shortchanged with Black President stuff. With Obama's last-minute efforts to create road blocks for the newly elected President with Israel and Russia fake news diversionary messages, it was doubtful if another black man may be trusted as President of America for a long time.

It would be very conclusive to conclude the series with the following words on President Obama, he made history as the first black President, unfortunately, he did not fulfill the dreams of Martin Luther king Jr. or what was the purpose of history he made, if it cannot open the doors for other black politicians to get to the same level like him? Obama probably through his actions and inactions closed door and it may take a long time to open.

President Barack Hussein Obama who after second term was thinking of third term through Hillary which was not in the Constitution and when he failed, he made sure his successor had problems, that would be how to assess Obama and his third term dream through Hillary Clinton and when he failed, the Obasanjo in him came out with his last-minute executive orders.

Somehow, he was not the only one who thought of third term Hillary Clinton's husband Bill Clinton said he would like to ride the Airforce One plane again as first man or so and both were disappointed and frustrated with the outcome of the election.

(23)

Israel

We saw how and why both President Obama and Prime Minister Netanyahu threw jabs at themselves openly to the happiness of the enemies of the two nations. Israel was almost like the unmentioned 51st state of the United States of America far away like Hawaii the 50th state.

Israel harbors the best brain of America inventors from Cell Phone to Space ventures the cooperation between the two nations including the cover up democracy in the Middle East was not what anyone with the love for Islam based on the principle of Ottoman Empire was or was happy about.

Let us restore the old glory of our people had always been in the mind of everyone in the Middle East if you were a Muslim you would want the Ottoman and Persians back. It was the reason the Muslim brotherhood was founded. If you were Jewish, King David might, and glory would be your dream, to the Old United States of America for its glory and restoration of the great Temple built by his son King Solomon.

Islam was a religion that could not exist without the history of the Jews and their Kings and prophets, it was also a religion that could not be sanctified without the stories in the Christian Bible and Jewish Torah and somehow, the Quranic version of the stories both in Torah and Bible did not totally support what Quran mentioned about Jewish history.

Each day the believer in Quran sees the Jews differently, it was like being looked at by a person who could puncture your story or religion with their own facts. I have in the past questioned what would the Quran look like if it did not contain the stories in Torah and Bible? I couldn't see it.

While the Muslims relied on the stories of Angel Gabriel to Prophet Mohamed as the story of God (Allah) and Jews unfortunately for the Muslims, the Bible and Torah recorded their own history with facts and figures and the Angel Gabriel in the Bible did not tell the same stories about God in the same way the Mohamed version of the Angel Gabriel did.

The above was the reason why Israel must never be freed. Her freedom was a revelation of questions the Muslim world would always be uncomfortable with including their spiritual places.

By the time the British returned the Jews back to their Biblical home, the Muslims world became uncomfortable because her freedom from everyone and spiritual freedom would give them the right to tell the world their stories not what any Angel told anyone or any other religion.

(24)

By February 20th, 2017 officially President Trump would have been a month straight old on the job as President of the most powerful nation on earth and during his less than a month in office he took the bull by the horn with almost 20 executive others to re-shape US Foreign and domestic policies.

Unfortunately, President Trump made a vital mistake, he failed to keep his adversaries busy with Hillary Clinton's problem on email leaks and hidden server with that his adversaries became stronger than expected hopefully this coming week Mr. Trump would strategize and keep the Democrats busy with problems to enable him focus on his own agenda to make America great again.

One of the historical mistakes of President Trump would be his pick for Attorney General Former Senator Jeff Session from Alabama State, he became a very reluctant associate to protect his presidency. After eight years of Democrats in the White House it was almost impossible to assume the loyalty of those employed in last eight years was not to the government and policies of Barrack Hussein Obama.

And that was where President Trump failed to quickly understand when Bush 43 became President he knew at least majority of the problems and traps the eight years of Bill Clinton would be, he took all the previous personnel of his father Bush 41 to manage the White House for him and despite all those precautions 9/11 still happened, in case of Trump he had none of it from the past to help his infant presidency

When Barrack Obama became President in 2009 he took most of the staffs of Bill Clinton to help his infant administration luckily for him, because of the recession and free fall of the economy, it was difficult for then President George Bush even if he had any intention to add more to the problems of President Obama who had made a secret pact with the 42th President Bill Clinton to help his wife succeed him.

Bill Clinton wanted Hillary for Vice President but that was rejected at the primaries to prevent a repeat of what happened to President Kennedy in 1963.

Senator J F Kennedy had taken his bitter opponent in the Democrats Primaries L B Johnson of Dallas Texas as his VP and when President Kennedy visited Dallas in 1963, he was killed, it was that reason Obama did not pick Hillary as Vice President in 2008.

It was a kind of life Insurance for the first black President instead he took Joe Biden a harmless and likeable Senator as his Vice President, in American politics after President, VP And Speaker of the House, the next powerful office was Secretary of State and it was what Obama offered Hillary Clinton with the hope she would be out of the country for most of the time to prevent what happened between Jimmy Carter and Senator Kennedy when Carter wanted second term.

It was Senator Ted Kennedy of Massachusetts who challenged President Jimmy Carter and lost before he lost to President Ronald Reagan

Hillary Clinton would allow Obama to run his two terms and Hillary would use the last four years of Obama to consolidate for 2016 meaning, Hillary Clinton would not face any serious competition from Democrats, at least that was the plan until Independent Senator Bernie Sanders of Vermont came from nowhere to destroy the secret pact plan for the assumed first woman President that would crack the walls.

The above was the foundation of the relationship between Clinton and Obama with the hope after eight years of Hillary his own wife, his smart and his former boss Michelle in the law firm would be President.

The rest was history; President Trump an outsider thought he too could run the White House in a different way outside how Bill Clinton, George Bush and Barrack Obama avoided leaks from the White House with his own loyalists the little knowledge of inside White House politics, the leak had claimed Trump's most trusted National Security Adviser Gen Mike Flynn for talking to the Russian before Trump became President as if Hillary did not talk to the Chinese and Saudi Arabia infact Huma Abideen the right-hand lady of Hillary Clinton was very close to the Muslim radical organization in Saudi Arabia.

Until President cleans the House more would come out that would almost destroy his presidency. It was no use for him making noise about the Press or media they would never be his friend and every day they were hoping for a scandal to blow away his presidency for many reasons. CNN, MSNBC, NBC, ABC, and Washington Post all hated Trump with vengeance for his presidency to survive he had to hold onto his weapon.

One of them was the use of modern day technology like Twitter and Facebook to cut off their bread and butter as the source of information.

Secondly except for Fox news that was established in 1995 or so to defend conservative ideals the rest were liberals and were owned by democrats and New York Times was practically owned by a guy from Mexico. CNN ABC and MSNBC would never write anything good until his presidency was impeached.

The option was for Trump to take the fight to them reopens Hillary case on Emails and others with that he could keep his words otherwise the midterm elections may not be fine in the House for him.

(25)

General Flynn

That General Flynn lost his job as National Security Adviser because of his meeting on the phone with Russian Ambassador before Trump became the President was no longer news.

At the time of the meeting, all the Hillary Clinton's crew including Former President Bill Clinton met with the Chinese Ambassador just like Gen Flynn met with the Russians. It was difficult to understand why nations would not meet whoever was running for the highest post in America, every nation wanted to position itself into the good book of any new administration and Russia which suffered lots of sanctions from Obama's administration could not be expected to stand aloof in the US Presidential election.

The team that won the election became the victim of the meetings before the election. It was not clear if an appointee of Hillary Clinton would have been removed like Gen Flynn was treated, General Michael Flynn problem started before his trip to Russia, he was the assistant to the General Barrack Obama removed after the later granted with Rolling Stone magazine He was the head of Defense Intelligence who was pushed out after series of clashes over his leadership styles, Washington Post wrote on General Flynn as a former Intelligence officer under General McChrystal in Iraq and Afghanistan who was himself fired by President Obama over his controversial interview with the Rolling Stones magazines, he was replaced by General David, H Petraeus, and his removal led to outside post of his staff and one of them was Lt General Michael Flynn.

It was even reported that General Flynn management style was very aggressive, he pushed for changes without adequate follow through.

In 2014 he announced he was leaving after 35 years of service, same said, he did not do a good job as the head of DIA, however, President Obama administration Jimmy Giant reported he was fired for insubordination, for failure to follow orders of his superiors however, General Flynn gave a different version he felt he was fired because he took a tougher actions on Islamic terrorists, whatever, it was the reason he gave for his job lost under President Obama, it could not be ruled out from lack of respect for his superiors and how Obama fired his boss, General McChrystal.

A former agency officer and a General Flynn supporter said he said he wanted to take advantage of the budget pressure which made him to demand a new approach from DIA bloated bureaucracy with the overstaff and it was why he was a danger to the status quo.

In 2010 General Michael Flynn had written a scathing and detailed report titled "Fixing Intel" in the report he mentioned how irrelevant military intelligence it was to the task of counter insurgence campaign in Afghanistan and one could wonder who was his boss then, if not the same General McChrystal who did not show respect for President Obama.

If in future President Obama was not happy if he had a future and a career with his successor as a threat on would not be surprised, meanwhile Former President Barack Obama was running a network of insiders in the White House leaking information to him and leaking it to Press to undermine Trump's Presidency they were called shadow warriors.

Trump's administration had identified 90 of such workers and would be shown the exit doors next week. Senator Rand Paul looked at President Trump's administration and said this. Donald Trump was a President who confronts the narratives while regular politicians go with the narratives.

President Trump was just different from us, he was captivating more like what you want to see every day on television. And to his credit he gets things done.

President Trump was talking directly to the people and visiting factories on his message of Made in UNITED STATES OF AMERICA.

In a related news Ford motor made a U Turn it would no longer move a division of its manufacturing company to Mexico, the company was staying right here in United States of America.

Despite the noise of the Liberals President Trump was willing to meet with Congressional black caucus CBC to discuss how the African Americans can be helped in the development going on but they were not showing interest, can you blame them?

Probably why?

They were mostly Democrats and if you ask them what Democrats did for the blacks in the last 50 years with 39% of those in jail were blacks, 58% unemployed youths, largest school dropout and mostly behind in Math's and English language they have nothing to show for it, like Trump said what the hell do they have to lose? Could Trump run his government without the Blacks with just 14% US population?

Yes.

I think the African Americans must show interest in a government extending hands of fellowship to them we have nothing to lose, otherwise they could be left behind as president

Trump was looking for a fresh start and allies to run his government.

(26)

Sometimes it was better to stay with one's gut feelings to get away from trouble. Donald Trump was right until the GOP convinced him to hire Paul Manafort as his new Campaign Manager because his first campaign Manager Corey Lewandowski (43) was relatively too young and vibrant without a stronghold on the establishment ready to form a collation that could get Trump the much-needed delegates against the hostile group of the Party at the Ohio Convention of the Republican Party.

If the New York Billionaire Donald Trump, a new face into presidential dream must win the support of GOP, he needed an insider like Paul Manafort to do the healings of the Party for him.

Paul was 67 years old, with BA, JD from Georgetown University, the guru of US Politics and adviser to all Republican Past Presidents since Gerald Ford, Reagan, George H Bush inclusive and consultants/ lobbyist to most dictators around the world like Mobutu Sese Seko of Zaire, Ferdinand Marco of Philippines, Jona Savinbi of Angola and Viktor Yanukovych of Ukraine those were some of his clients, his political resume was too heavy to ignore.

Paul eyes were something to behold, he could make you change your religion or spouse with a gifted power to hypnotize anyone. Paul was the campaign Manager of the doyen of the GOP late President Reagan in the eighties who secured the delegates for the Gipper and a win against President Jimmy Carter the peanut favor President from Georgia who was running for second term. If anybody could put the Republican Party behind Donald Trump and get him to secure the required delegates on first ballot, it must be Paul.

Donald Trump reluctantly caved in to the pressure of the Party that never really loved him; he had to show the GOP he could be trusted. His first Campaign Manager Corey was eased out to work for CNN to defend Trump with his greatest media enemies, that singular action would become a problem that would in future tainted his presidency.

Unknown to candidate Trump, his new Campaign Manager Paul Manafort had a baggage of problems from his post Reagan days as a Consultant and Lobbyist to the disgraced President of Ukraine Viktor Yanukovych which he never fully disclosed his past to his new employer Candidate Trump.

Paul was probably a mafia if not the head of it. If you needed a clean cut dirty job in politics talk to Paul was the statement from the underground. Paul in the past had always outsmarted the CIA, FBI, MSS, ODIN and Fin Cen and they had nothing on him. He was dirty, more like a man who covered his dirt with colors.

Politics is not a game for the angels neither it was a job of the open criminals only those who could stridulously hide everything between the truth and ugly could survive the game of politics. Paul's connection to Ukraine which was in good note with Russia until the politics of Ukraine became pro NATO and EU and both nations fell apart.

Eventually, Russian invaded Ukraine and grabbed what was traditionally Russian land Crimea and the previous President of Ukraine Viktor Yanukovych was found to be corrupt and all his friends including Paul were pro Russia by New Pro West government in Ukraine.

President Obama administration had to use her failed policies in Asia which Russia outnumbered him as an excuse to push for economic sanctions against Russia did the obviously Paul gave out the weapon they needed against Trump.

Paul was paid under the table for his job because most third world nations were corrupt he could only declare the very little he could and when he was exposed, Trump had to let him go not until he had delivered the delegates Trump needed and assurance of the GOP behind Trump.

Trump had more to chew than to be saddled with Paul's problem, he quickly elevated Kelly Anne Conway as the first female campaign Manager and he put Paul behind. How could he get rid of the US political mafia head without running into trouble himself?

Did he?

In politics, the past was not easy to push aside, it was a package you carry along for the rest of you career, Paul's connection became the link for the liberal to destroy the smiles on the face of Trump after he strategically defeated Hillary Clinton.

Paul as Campaign Manager was genius, out of the six strategically battleground states and blue states he lined up for Trump to win only Connecticut failed to be in the tent of Trump. He knew Hillary Clinton was careless just like her emails with some blue states in the North, like Michigan and Wisconsin. He knew everything and with Steve Bannon. He knew Trump could strategically win if he stayed on his message and like a kid both made sure Trump stayed on message.

If politics of presidential dream was a religion, Paul Manafort and Steve Bannon could be the Bible of it, Trump read both men like the holy book and followed whatever they recommended and when Steve Bannon told candidate Trump to let go of Paul he did not question his judgment. He knew Steve could do the job alone. Steve Bannon and Paul Manafort were business partners and even movie partners along with Davis and Freedman, when the game was up for Paul Manafort there was no need for him to hang around anymore, besides the agenda of President Trump was more than the baggage of Manafort had around.

---

(27)

The politics of Obamacare

Affordable Health Care Act known as Obamacare was designed in good faith by President Obama to care for 47 million Americans that had no medical insurance, however, it was used by less than 22 million Americans thereby fell short of premium and crowd to make it viable among other mandates in the ACA.

After seven years of government subsidizing the program it became a monster rather than the honest intentions the Bill was meant to attain.

Between 1965-1968 through Senator Ted Kennedy after he successfully got the Medicare and Medicaid Bill on he came up with the idea of healthcare for all like Canada and other nations in

Europe however, President Bill Clinton took the idea in 1992 and named it after his wife Hillary and with the careless way it was handled it never became the law.

At a time, Senator Ted Kennedy ran for President against incumbent President Carter in the DNC primaries in the eighties, the program which would in future be called Obamacare was the core of his campaign. He lost the primaries to the incumbent President Jimmy Carter, who on the long run lost the Presidency to President Ronald Reagan of California.

By the time, President Obama introduced the Bill which needed 60 Senators to make it law of the land, Senators Kennedy was on the stage four Cancer and from the hospital bed he was wheeled to the Senate to give the Bill his vote. It was the happiest moment for Ted Kennedy and best wishes for him who had endorsed Obama over Hillary in 2007 primaries of the Democrats.

Both Obama and Clinton should never have named the Bills after themselves other than the Affordable Healthcare Act what it was called should not have allowed the GOP to name it as such. It should have been called Kennedy-care the Lion of the Senate, the

Senator with input in all the healthcare system in America because of the sickness in his family both nuclear and extended families.

Ted Kennedy the last of the three Kennedy's including Robert Kennedy killed in California in 1968 and President J F Kennedy who was assassinated in Dallas Texas in 1963 did more for America in healthcare than any person in the history of the nation. He introduced Wheelchairs into all the hospitals and Nursing homes in America.

The above was just a brief history of the ACA. if it was a good program as it was meant to be it was however done with selfish intentions, the organizer meaning the DNC did not include the value of America as a capitalist nation in the Bill they reasoned like socialist and that offended the GOP.

Democrats eroded the right to choose in the Bill, it gave too much power to the government than the patient, it became the final arbiter on who and what could be done on healthcare and somehow, the program shot itself in the legs with the penalty code in the law which made it possible to pay as little as $600 fine if one chooses not to partake in the program and it became the route most people took since average premium was about $4800 as against $600, and who would not?

Obamacare was designed to help the women more than men, it went deeper into all their medical problems, from annual breast check, to their reproduction organs and planned parenthood which became a beneficiary of the generous program, contraception was highlighted, and It offended the Catholic church and some institutions based on faith.

Obamacare was also good to those with pre-existing health problems like cancer or degenerative diseases as no insurance company could deny anyone from enrollment in addition, those under 26 years could remain under their parent's health insurance. It was more of a socialist program. And again, strange to a country based on capitalism.

The children also benefited from the program, it did not make provision for illegal immigrants except on emergency room treatment.

As generous and as very humane Obamacare looked on paper why did it fail?

It did not get enough people as planned into the program, the shortage of 27 million subscribers made the program dependent more on government subsidies, it did not negotiate the cost of the same drug sold in Europe and South America and that became the problem, meaning, a $2 drug in Europe could be $20 America. Why? most of the Congress men were under the control of the lobbyists controlled by the pharmaceutical companies. Instead of reducing cost, the result was the opposite.

Because of uncontrollable cost most insurance companies pulled out of the program and those who stayed increased the premium as much as 500%, many took advantage of the System, honestly Obamacare was abused by those who knew the system.

Out of 3178 counties in America about a third of the figures lost their Obamacare as insurance pulled out and the future of a celebrated healthcare system looked bleaker than anyone could imagine.

Note, at the time Obamacare was signed no single Republican voted in support of it and it was repealed in the House several times under the former Speaker but could not get to the

Senate floor and Supreme court gave the law the legs to stand with the GOP could not forgive Justice John Robert for his Supreme Court vote which gave Obamacare the only life Line, to penalize those who failed to sign for it under comer Law.

(28)

2016 ELECTION ON OBAMACARE

It became the most important topic for the campaign, it was a monster Hillary Clinton the Democrats nominee had to embrace whether she Like it or not, Obama Care with President Obama still in office was difficult her to run away from and that includes the assets and liabilities of the program.

At a time when her husband former President Bill Clinton read the hand written on the wall to cleverly steer Hillary away from a disaster called Obamacare, it was too late, and Hillary inherited the ugly side of the program because of cost Americans like any other people on earth closed their eyes to the benefits of Obamacare as far as they were concerned Obamacare was the same as Hillary-care or more like Siamese. And it was difficult for her to separate her policy the program she had earlier claimed as Obamacare in the past.

Republican candidate Donald Trump campaigned against the program and he focused more on its shortcoming rather than the good side of it. He used Obama's sales talk on the program to weaken Hillary Clinton. "Keep your Doctor and program" as mentioned by President Obama which did not happen as planned.

Taxes attached to the program weakened it more, it helped it. The called it Cadillac taxes on medical devices for local and external created more than was planned. Obamacare is ready to implode they all say, and when would that happen? The National Debt under President Obama went from $11.6 trillion in his eight years in office to $21 trillion became a concern.

Was it possible to cancel and replace Obamacare? No. It could only be fine turned to make it possible with the capitalistic tendency of the country.

Why Republicans pulled the GOP Bill out? It had not full proof alternative to Obamacare with a socialist tendency, when a program was almost seven years old in the market, it was not easy to stop could the immediate words to describe it.

GOP controlled House got disorganized by those making money from the System and about 32 GOP in the House facing re-election in 2018 got the messages from their donors and consistencies not to stay away from it if they still wanted to return to the House in 2018.

The pundit believed the GOP Bill would come back but when was the question and if it would, a cooperation of both parties would be required to fix and not to repeal, the Oracle says Obamacare is here in America like other social benefits.

(29)

Sanctuary Cities War with Federal Government starts all over the country. (1)

To start with, let it be known, if you over stay your visa in any country particularly the United States of America, it was not a criminal offense per the law of the land, it was a civil case and to circumvent this from being used as a criminal case for political reasons, sanctuary cities emerged to protect undocumented immigrants which the US law called illegal aliens.

However, a Sanctuary city was more than a haven for undocumented immigrants in the country, it was a City most criminals not found the support of the local Police and noncompliance in helping the Federal Government to enforce the law of the land on illegal immigrants with criminal records and those the law asked to leave the country and most of them were spread all over the nation and they were mostly controlled by the Liberal or democrats.

Because of this, former President Obama in office who deported more than 2.5 million illegal immigrants could not implement the law fully to make the cities in compliance with Federal Government on immigration laws with ICE, note, the law against Sanctuary Cities was not signed by President Trump.

However, sanctuary Cities motive in the recent years moved beyond the earlier objective of protection, it was also used to protect criminals among the illegal aliens and it was difficult to separate the totality of the good from the ugly side of the benefits of it or as against a program to improve the health and school enrollment among other social benefits, that could attract Federal funding.

The Republican Party on the other hand was mostly anti Sanctuary City for the reverse reasons of the Democrats, because it would not benefit from the long-term effect of the immigrants when they eventually adjust their immigration status.

Why?

If Most of the beneficiaries of Sanctuary Cities would end up as Democrats, why not stop them could be the untold and hidden stories behind it.

Sanctuary cities in fact were used as nursing homes for democrat's expansion over the Republican Party membership drive and growth in the country and with the way it was organized it could be the haven of illegal voting since the records of the cities involved could not be verified or they would not comply with the system.

Most of the Sanctuary Cities would not cooperate to have voter's identification in any election, if the Bank, or driving a car or even flying by air would require identification why not voters?

The Democrats would not agree particularly in the counties with Sanctuary Cities and it made them a suspect if the allegations of voter's fraud could be the reasons why Democrats were getting more than the Republicans which made the electoral college the only saving grace for the Republican Party to win election which was what happened in the last Presidential election with over three million votes by Hillary Clinton over the eventual winner President Donald Trump. Her votes came from the Sanctuary cities.

Out of the 3237 Counties in America, Hillary Clinton only secured her voted from only 500 plus counties the rest went to President Trump, meaning all the so-called three million popular voted came from highly undocumented sanctuary cities like New York, Los Angeles and in most cases New York Police department NYPD and LA Police blocked Federal ICE from touching undocumented immigrants in the schools unless they could obtain a court order.

All the Mayors of Sanctuary Cities were more like a Union now against the law President Obama signed but failed to implement as Trump was dusting the book as law and order government and General Kelly the Secretary in charge of Homeland Security would be meeting the Mayors of all the US Cities for cooperation and compliance with the Federal Government over illegal immigrants they harbor in their counties or cities

As a first step towards compliance, the Federal government announced through Attorney General Jeff Session, that Fed would stop Funding all the Sanctuary Cities, and how would these cities take this policy of the Central government? Some would attempt to go to Court which may not be the best option if President Trump Supreme Court nominee was confirmed and it was one of the hidden reason the Democrats were dragging their feet over the confirmation of Justice Neil Gorsuch as an Associate Justice of the nine members of the Supreme Court of the United States of America

(30)

SUPREME COURT

In the book "The Nine: Inside the secret world of US Supreme Court " written solely to explain why US operates with nine Supreme Court Justices, the author Jeffrey Tobin a journalist and regular commentator on CNN made it clear the Constitution did not peg the numbers of Supreme Justice to 9.

Nine was a figure the nation evolved to after several years of trying different numbers, at one time, the numbers in the Supreme were up to 15, 13 and 11 until 9 became the members that could stand the test of time and it could change in future, meaning, a Liberal President and a liberal Congress could change the numbers from 9 to whatever if the plan is to change or weaken the Constitution in view of global doctrines creeping into the country.

A President could stamp his legacy for 25 years or more with his Supreme court nominee. On the Supreme Court bench those appointed by President Reagan and Bush 41 were still presiding and more than 25 years ago.

Justice Anthony Kennedy was appointed by President Reagan 29 years ago, Clarence Thomas 26 year, [Bush 41] Ruth Ginsburg 24yrs, Stephen Breuer 23yrs, [Clinton] Justice John Robert 12yrs, Samuel Alito 11yrs [Bush 43] Justice SONIA Sotomayor 8yrs, Elena Kagan 7yrs. [Obama]

If President Barrack Obama made a mistake in his eight years in office, it could be his inability to nominate a black Supreme Court Justice that could take care of his race since Justices Clarence Thomas, an appointee of President Bush 41 married to a White woman never really showed interest in the black problems in the country and as it is now, it may right to say the African Americans do not have a voice in the Supreme Court, this is the bitter truth.

When Justice Anthony Scalia the most conservative and the heart of the Republican Party voice in the Supreme court died about early in 2016, it was a big blow to the Republican Party and to allow President Obama to fill his seat with a liberal Justice in the year of election would have been an end to conservative ideas in America politics.

The above could indicate, something that would be difficult to amend at least for the next twenty five years, meaning, the Constitution could be technically amended with pronouncements of the court in favor of liberalism, even Hillary Clinton could have been challenged the result of the last elections in favor of the popular votes as against the electoral college and a liberal Supreme Court could do anything if Obama had his way with his third nominee before the Republican Controlled Senate denied his request.

The Republican Party was right to insist on waiting until after Presidential elections before the winner could appoint a replacement for Justice Scalia, a lot was on the line, if Donald Trump had lost election, Hillary Clinton in office for eight years would have sent the GOP into perdition. it was indeed a big gamble which eventually paid off

As of now, the effect of eight years of Obama could be seen from all the circuit judges ruling against President Trump executive order, in his first year in office they were appointed by President Obama after the 60 confirmation votes in the Senate was destroyed for Nuclear option and to add eight years of another Democrats President to it would have been too much to predict the future of America founded on Christian and Judaism values, the country was going South and election of Donald J Trump saved or postponed the massive attack the Liberal wanted on the US Constitution over global doctrines.

President Trump nominee Judge Neil Gorsuch with over 2700 cases on his resume, and Associate Law Professor, a judge described almost a clone of his mentor, late Justice Antonio Scalia from the composition of the Senate he may be the first Supreme Court Justice to be confirmed by simple majority, otherwise called Nuclear Option.

Neil Gorsuch on April 10th, 2017 was confirmed, and he took his oath of office as an associate of the Supreme Court

The ball was in the court of the frustrated Democrats in the Senate, they could tuck in their pride and confirm Justice Neil Gorsuch or destroy the system like they did with other appointments in the lower courts, whatever they do, plus or minus, Justice Gorsuch would be confirmed that was the consensus of the 52 Republican Senators with or without eight other Neil Gorsuch was confirmed as an Associate Justice of the Supreme Court by a simple majority 56/42. His main duty would be to continue with the legacy of late Justice Antonio Scalia. Neil was born in August 296h 1967 from Denver Colorado.

The confirmation of Justice Neil Gorsuch would be another legacy of President Trump in his first year in office

(31)

Russia in the House

On paper, the dissolution of the old USSR was a regrettable policy of Gorbachev, the 8th and last Leader of the old Soviet Union who had moved into the Kremlin as the General Secretary of the Communist Party. He worked on Glasnost (openness) and perestroika (restructuring) of the Party of Lenin but the weight of the party's influence was too strong for him to provide effective leadership.

Hence, Gorbachev removed the party internal control from the political administration of the government, the negativity of it outweighs the positive effect of his actions or in-actions, it became the foundation for the end of cold war and dissolution of the powerful USSR was the only option.

However, to those outside the inner workings of the Kremlin, it was the 40th President of the United States of America late Ronald Reagan who succeeded in cajoling the last USSR leader Gorbachev to dismantle the country after a massive failure economically and politically. It was when USSR became too much of a burden to run.

Furthermore, it could be said not all Citizens of USSR agreed with the dissolution decision that reluctantly gave freedom to new nations out of USSR and Russia went back to what it was before the Russia revolution to being as a smaller and bitter nation just as United States of America emerged as the most powerful nation on earth, with no country on earth to challenge her.

And whatever was the fear earlier expressed in the West. RUSSIA was no longer a threat but a nation in search for a new direction while UNITED STATES OF AMERICA massively carried the burden of the world with no Russia around to share or split. With that, it was the policy of the White House to spread democracy to all the nations with that old USSR got clipped.

Boris Yeltsin a drunk took over from Gorbachev since Gorbachev's mandate was over USSR he could not be transferred to a new Russia and he was busy struggling with the past or reactions of the dissolution than rebuilding the new nation. Yeltsin became the man and a friend of the West.

It was difficult for Gorbachev to assume Russia would take his Presidency as given until he got clipped and could not make a comeback despite all the funny awards given to him by the western nation, it was more a glorification of his failures and that of USSR than the freedom he talked about and between Yeltsin and Putin no other President emerged while Yeltsin operated with eight Prime Ministers during his administration, Putin was indeed the last or one of the Prime ministers Yeltsin groomed for the future.

Putin was a conservative old Russian block a Colonel of the KGB and in his heart who still craved for the old USSR if only he could turn back the clock.

The first two terms of President Putin in Russia at the time Bush was US President he gave the America the upper edge it needed which made Russia to look the other way when America invaded Iraq. Note the agreement with Saddam Hussein was like what President Assad of Syria had with Russia.

When Putin stepped down to become the Prime Minister, his surrogate Dmitri Medvedev became the President, it was glaring he was dancing round the constitution for a comeback and President Obama never liked the idea of a Putin in the world politics despite calling the shots as the Prime Minister.

The 2012 election in Russia was the year America under President Obama and Secretary of State Hillary Clinton got involved in Russia election.

Hillary Clinton State Department teamed up with Golos. and independent organization for election monitoring for ten years to work against the comeback strategy of the Prime Minister Putin.

However, to those outside the inner workings of the Kremlin, it was the 40th President of the United States of America Ronald Reagan who succeeded in cajoling the last USSR leader

Gorbachev to dismantle the country after a massive failure economically and politically.

Furthermore, it could be said not all Citizens of USSR agreed with the dissolution decision that reluctantly gave freedom to new nations out of USSR and Russia went back to what it was before the Russia revolution as a smaller and bitter nation just as UNITED STATES OF AMERICA emerged as the most powerful nation on earth.

At the same time, it was difficult for Gorbachev to assume Russia would take his Presidency as given until he got clipped and could not make a comeback despite all the funny awards given to him by the western nations, it was more a glorification of his failures and that of USSR, than the freedom he talked about and between Boris Yeltsin and Vladimir Putin, no other President emerged while Yeltsin operated with eight Prime Ministers during his administration, Putin was indeed the last or one of the Prime ministers Yeltsin groomed for the future.

Putin was a conservative old Russian block, and a Colonel of the KGB and in his heart who still craved for the old USSR if only he could turn back the clock.

The first two terms of President Putin in Russia at the time Bush was US President gave the United states of America, the upper edge it needed which made Russia to look the other way when America invaded Iraq. Note the agreement with Saddam Hussein was like what President Assad of Syria had with Russia.

When Putin became the Prime Minister of with his surrogate Dmitri Medvedev as the President it was glaring he was dancing round the constitution for a comeback and President Obama never liked the idea of a Putin in the world politics despite calling the shots as the Prime Minister.

(32)

Ukraine Connection

Those expecting the Russians to back away from Crimea peninsula in Ukraine must not be students of history or they must be blind to a war which had a history dated back to October 1853 to February 1856 which almost half a million-people died, mostly, Russians over what was called the Crimean war which, Britain, France and Ottoman Empire destroyed the might of Russian Empire in the Crimean Peninsula.

It was a battle that was fought over the control of the Black sea and Azov Sea to check mate Russia and its communication with the rest of the Europe from the sea port of Sevastopol and every attempt for Russia to expand was put on hold with the treaty of Paris of March 1856. Over ten battles could be found over this peninsula, like the Battle of Serov, Battle of Alma, Battle of Sevastopol etc. until the Yalta Conference of 1927 between the Russian Dictator, Joseph Stalin, American President Franklin D Roosevelt, and British Prime Minister Winston Churchill.

President of Russia Vladimir Putin

In 1921 most of the ethnic Tartar group mostly Muslims and pro-western government of today were deported from then USSR by Joseph Stalin, however, in 1954 since Ukraine was part of USSR it did not matter what was the fate of Crimean peninsula, for administrative purpose this hard earned territory of Russia with blood of almost 750,000 Russian preceding the creation of Soviet leader Nikita Khrushchev a native of Ukraine gave the area to his native land of Ukraine, until 1991 when Ukraine became an independent state as a result of the dissolution of USSR under Gorbachev the need to question the gift of Nikita Khrushchev of the Crimea to Ukraine became necessary and Russian the original owner of the peninsula became an Indian giver, the question is if the nation would be justified to ask Crimean be given back to the country of Russian for symbolical blood of those lost in the 1953-1856 wars?

The above, is just a tip on the ice bag on why Russian would never give up on that part of Ukraine which the history, tradition, culture and might of United Nations veto power gave the nation of Russia an edge over others, today 58 percent of those living there were Russians, moreover, before the dissolution of USSR it was and still the center for all the war fleets of old Soviet Union now Russian Federation, the rest of the population, 24 percent were from Ukraine natives and 12 percent were Tartar that may be deported like Dictator Joseph Stalin did in 1927 or be killed under President Putin, a potential refugees for the western world.

Secondly, Russian President Putin belongs to the old blog who still believes President Gorbachev was wrong to have allowed President Ronald Reagan of United States of America to have used his famous speech "Tear that wall down" which led to the dissolution of USSR, President Putin, if he could have his way he would turn the hands of the clock back to what it was with all the breakaway countries back into the tight hands of Russia as USSR again.

Thirdly, the Oracle asked what is in there in Crimea for Russia federation? More than just a dream, it is the realty, control of the Baltic sea since 1856 treaty of Paris over Sea of Azov and Black Sea, free **access to** the European Markets, and a strong military presence to match the United States of America control of the region in Turkey, a strong foothold into the Mediterranean sea and a gradual return to the cold war which Gorbachev was never forgiven by the conservatives led by the President Putin in a new war strategies in which America economy may be too weak to stand another war to defend Europe like it did in the first and second world wars.

Fourthly, Russia government under Putin would never give up this time around over Crimean, because the time is right for the dreams of Russian to win back what it gave away in 1945 to Ukraine as a region of USSR then, but when US Secretary of State.

President Petrov Poroshenko of Ukraine

John Kerry and his Russian counterpart met for six hours, the Oracle was wondering what they were talking about, since the body language of Russian and it military presence was an indication the meeting was just a waste of time for Russian to execute the final plan to merge Crimean back to Russian, it is like asking Britain to give up the Falkland when it went to war with Argentina, or for the American government to give up its influence over Puerto Rico in future.

Furthermore, behind all these epistles were the politics of manipulation of oil and gas industry and military might of Russia which would further exact might and presence of Russian Federation in the region, note this point from the Oracle, no amount of sanctions, military or otherwise could stop Russia from taking Crimean out of Ukraine, if the referendum fails to approve the take over Russia under President Putin a disciple of old USSR would take it by force.

United State of America, Secretary of State Kerry said, it would amount to back door annexation, but the Oracle would like the former Secretary to refer to history, to support his assertion, however, the ongoing over the referendum is just a smokescreen for the actions of Russia the annexation was done several decades ago in 1945 the current one is just a confirmation of what happened in the past, Crimea peninsula is home to what it was in 1945 part of

Russia. would Russia care what and how the rest of the world or NATO feels about the takeover, time would tell but if the body language of Russia is an indication of what to expect the Oracle feels the President Putin did not give a damn.

Former President Barack Hussein Obama

The Oracle would like to state here for historical purposes by next week, Crimea peninsula, that vital of Ukraine would be just another Region within Russia Federation and by this time next year no one would mention it again.

Which is the way politics is played among the Super Powers and a lesson for all the breakaway countries still having some of the goldmine of old USSR, like a pound of flesh Russia under President Putin may be knocking their doors again and again. As predicted, the Russian had her way with Crimea and the new administration of President Trump is left with messy diplomatic relations former President Barack Obama created with his inability to study history of how Crimea became part of Ukraine and how Russia decided in her wisdom or otherwise to revisit the Crimean deal after Ukraine pulled out of old USSR and romancing with NATO members with the objective of destroying the might of Russia in the Baltic Sea and a threat to her Submarines.

The Oracle would predict President Trump would not revisit the ugly mess of the past, his administration needs Russia for another mission on China, North Korea and Iran getting involve with Ukraine problem over Crimean was nothing but a distraction for this administration, time to move on.

(33)

Post- Election analyses

Why Democrats lost the State of Michigan with its 18 electoral college votes to the Republican Donald Trump in 2016 election?

By 2008, Detroit the Motor City was a mess, the state of Michigan lost everything, most home owners left their properties because they could no longer pay their mortgage and when President Obama came he promised to help, however at the end of his presidency, he helped only the motor companies without the people and 2016 was the *pay back* for the neglect of 8 years of Obama presidency.

Even the city of Flint had the worst water in America and when Candidate Trump came they gave him their votes at least to try something new from Democrat that deceived them for almost 50 years.

Where was Russia in this! Like the Mexicans would say "Nada* Russia was an excuse to cover failure even the Mayor of Chicago Rob Manuel the first Chief of Staff of Obama first term knew this.

While President Trump was making America great overseas and re asserting and regaining the influence of his country in the Middle East his enemies like CNN ABC, NY Times, and Washington Post controlled by the Democrats were busy scheming problems at home, all these to undermine his presidency.

How would President Trump handle post foreign trip success at home which no news network mainstream media carried would depend on events that would be known next week?

Since CNN and ABC would not allow Americans to have access to the good work of their President overseas hence Trump is keeping his Twitter, Facebook and other social media and they must struggle for information from open place and thereby affects their revenue through commercials.

Only Fox News made money in commercials because they have access to the truth, at the Same time the loss of the Democrats could be associated with collapse of the Union in most of the Coal mining states, the effect of NAFTA and World Trade all made Democrat weaker.

(34)

Media War in America.

1927 was the first time a President addressed the nation on the Radio instead of the usual Press Conference in any part of world and it happened here in America. In 1947 would be the first time on Television in America, first Television presidential debate in the world was in 1960 between Senator Kennedy and the Vice President Nixon.

Bill Clinton through internet made it possible to seek questions from Americans during a debate. Barrack Obama, became known as the first Black Berry Presidential candidate with more than 6 million emails, he used it to defeat Senator John McCain in 2008.

President Trump will be the first United State President with the latest technology Twitter to communicate with Americans directly like his predecessors used what was modern at their time. The more a President neglects the traditional mainstream press with modern technology the more the news.

They were called the mainstream media which was another name for pressure group with intention to change America from the dreams of founding fathers in 1789 to foreign ideologies.

And their mission was to destroy or weaken the Constitution of the United States of America with what they feed the citizens. Only six companies in America oversee this ugly mission of control when President Clinton removed the law that prohibited monopoly in America and today, 1600 Newspapers, 1109 Magazines, 9000 Radio Stations, 1500 Television Stations, 2400 Publishers

All the above was controlled by 6 companies and they were all liberal minded. This is one of the wars President Trump is fighting with, all the 97 Bills signed into law s were not highlighted by the Press, they focused more on the negative side and in most cases used fake news to discredit the legitimacy of his presidency.

(35)

Why President Trump fired FBI Director

President Trump required his own appointees into key positions not those appointed by former President Obama that may not be totally loyal to him or his agenda, unfortunately, FBI Director James Comey though a Republican was appointed by Obama and he got confused when he failed to indict Hillary Clinton over email scandals. President Trump did the right thing he needed his own men to run the government, Comey was a mole.

Did President Trump use and dump FBI Director Comey?

_____

Not by Trump.

One could only conclude that James Comey allowed himself to be used by former President Obama on Hillary's case. You cannot eat your cake and still have it, Comey should have resigned after Trump won the election, unfortunately, he was too naïve to see it coming and it would be wrong for anyone to shed tears for him.

Why now were the questions from the fake news media and as if they wanted Trump to wait for three years like Obama did on Hillary Clinton's scandals.

Furthermore, the current Acting FBI Director too may be fired. He was appointed by Obama and his wife took donation from Democrats to run for office.

Under United States of America Constitution or law that established FBI, a President could fire anyone, and he is not bound by law to give any or no reason at all for actions or inactions.

(36)

Leaders don't lead from behind

When Samuel L Jackson as a Colonel who led the rescue mission into Yemen to evacuate the US Ambassador in the movie "The rules of engagement" was asked by his Sergeant what to do when the insurgents killed two of the US Marines.

The Colonel said, "Waste the Gademn motherfucker" that may be the statement that could reveal the heart of President Trump after President Assad crossed many lines with the use of chemicals on innocent kids and women not only that Assad bombed those admitted into the hospital to destroy evidence of Chemicals.

Almost 59 missiles launched from Tomahawk, a product of Raytheon Security company in America, the Navy hanger was first used in eighties under President Bush the 41st US President, and currently designed to send a message to Assad unlike Obama who even defended Russia and praised Assad on removal of Chemicals all which were found to be fake.

Obama 44th US President

The photographs here revealed the difference between former President Obama who did not sit on the driver's seat at a time Osama was killed and President Trump who sat on the seat as commander-in-Chief when Syria was attacked.

Leading from behind was a weak and timid style of the former President Obama which was unlike any American past Presidents as a leader of the free world.

Russia had denied involvement in chemical attacks and the world was happy with step President Trump took.

On February 2nd, 2017 two things happened in the United States of America, King of Jordan met with President Trump in the White House and both had a Press conference which revealed how flexible President Trump could be on international issues despite his macho political talks before he won the election in November 2016.

The two issues made an impact on the meetings between the two leaders, firstly, the role of Israel among the Arab nations in which the two states solution would involve Arab leagues with Jerusalem as the Capital of the two countries.

Secondly, Syria over the use of Chemicals on innocent women and children and the step which was alien to the campaign promises of candidate Trump for President.

The above may drag the United States of America deeper into the crises against President Assad remotely created by the failed policies of Hillary Clinton and President Obama from the funny " lead from behind" policy which swept through Arab nations of Libya, Tunisia, Egypt, Yemen and Syria which failed.

President Obama was pushed to realize the mistake of his actions or in actions in supporting the rebels against President Assad was nothing but empty threats as his administration was unable to fully arm the rebels as they were radicals in mind and spirit.

However, by the time Obama drew the red line it was nothing but empty red line threat as Russia who looked the other way despite the promise to Saddam Hussein in Iraq was not the same Russia in the case of Syria. Russia was ready for war.

President Obama realized he might have taken a very hasty decision otherwise it could have led to a direct war with Russia which had been avoided since Russia pulled out of Cuba in 1961 or so when JFK was President. Obama held back, and the rebels got disappointed they broke into two, refugees and ISIS.

President Trump would have both secret and open meetings with Russia the backbone of Syria strong man President Assad and How would this be done?

The Oracle says it must be a give and take process. A Russia sanctioned economically by President Obama over Ukraine land grab of Crimea would trade in Syria for a removal of the sanctions before Assad could be removed that would be the best option.

What would be the new US policy in the Middle East? As both nations despite oppositions are ready to work together.

(37)

The Border wall against Mexico

When candidate Trump opened his campaign in 2015 he called Mexicans uncomplimentary names and in the first year of his administration he took steps towards building wall that would prevent Mexico from sending rapists, criminals and drugs to his country with an imposing wall with all features that would discourage those with dishonest intentions coming to America at least by the thinking of his administration.

The Bid for the wall closed on March 29th, 2017 and by the end of the week the winners of the 2000 miles wall would be known surprisingly.

Democrats attacked the contractors that bided for the wall that would secure the country they all claim to love. What would the wall look like?

1. 30 feet tall

2. 6 feet underground deep to prevent tunneling it.

3. Physically imposing

4. Slippery wall to climb

5. At least 4 hrs. of work to break

6. It must withstand sledge hammer, car back chisel or battery-operated cutting tools.

7. The side facing US must be aesthetically pleasing in color and anti-climbing device.

8. The wall could be powered electrically meaning unlawful climbers would be electrocuted.

The devil they say was always in the details, as the bid was silent on the wall outlook on the Mexican side of the wall, but rumor heard it would be electrically controlled with radiation power of 15-20 feet radius

Trump's wall against Mexico temporarily ran into a change, President Trump needed a stronger man in the White House, it was not a surprise news when he recalled the Secretary for Homeland Security General Kelly as the new Chief of Staff and Priebus the former Chair of the Republican Party was let go.

And on December 6th, 2017, Kirtjen Nielsen assumed office as the new Homeland Secretary to replace Gen John Kelly with Elaine Duke as her Deputy.

Kirtjen graduated with a Law Degree from Georgetown University (BS) and University of Virginia (JB) and a Security expert, she previously served as John Kelly Chief of Staff, a former Special Assistant to President George Bush and Senior Director for prevention, preparedness at White House Homeland Security.

(38)

Russia in the House.

On paper, the dissolution of the old USSR was a regrettable policy of Gorbachev the 8th and last Leader of the old Soviet Union who had moved into the Kremlin as the General Secretary of the Communist Party. He worked on Glasnost (openness) and perestroika (restructuring) of the Party of Lenin but the weight of party was too strong for effective leadership.

Hence, Gorbachev removed the party from the political administration of the government, the negatives outweighs the positive effect of his action or in-actions it became the foundation for the end of cold war and dissolution of the powerful USSR.

However, to those outside the inner workings of the Kremlin, it was the 40th President of the United States of America Ronald Reagan who succeeded in cajoling the last USSR leader Gorbachev to dismantle the country after a massive failure economically and politically.

Furthermore, it could be said not all Citizens of USSR agreed with the dissolution decision that reluctantly gave freedom to new nations out of USSR and Russia went back to what it was before the Russia revolution as a smaller and bitter nation just as USA emerged as the most powerful nation on earth.

And whatever was the fear earlier expressed in the West. RUSSIA was no longer a threat but a nation in search for a new direction while USA massively carried the burden of the world with no Russia around to share or split. With that, it was the policy of the White House to spread democracy to all the nations old USSR got clipped.

Boris Yeltsin a drunk took over from Gorbachev since Gorbachev's mandate was over USSR he could not be transferred to Russia and he was busy struggling with the past or reactions of the dissolution than rebuilding the new nation. Yeltsin became the man and a friend of the West.

It was difficult for Gorbachev to assume Russia would take his Presidency as given until he got clipped and could not make a comeback despite all the phony awards given to him by the western nation, it was more a glorification of his failures and that of USSR than the freedom he talked about and between Yeltsin and Putin no other President emerged while Yeltsin operated with eight Prime Ministers during his administration, Putin was indeed the last or one of the Prime ministers Yeltsin groomed for the future.

Putin was a conservative Old Russian block a Colonel of the KGB and in his heart who still craved for the old USSR if only he could turn back the clock.

The first two terms of President Putin in Russia at the time Bush was US President gave the America the upper edge it needed which made Russia to look the other way when America invaded

Iraq. Note the agreement with Saddam Hussein was like what President Assad of Syria had with Russia.

When Putin became the Prime Minister of Russia with his surrogate Dmitri Medvedev as the President it was glaring he was dancing round the constitution for a comeback and President Obama never liked the idea of a Putin in the world politics despite calling the shots as the Prime Minister.

The 2012 election in Russia was the year America under President Obama and Secretary of State got involved in Russia election. Hillary Clinton's State Department teamed up with Golos and independent organization for election monitoring for ten years to work against the comeback strategy of the Prime Minister Putin.

(39)

The Politics of DACA

DACA Delayed Actions on children Actions or Dreamers or Deferred Children Actions or simply Development, Relief, Educational, Alien Minor Act, under Dreamer Act, the purpose of it was to stop deportation of children brought into the country illegally by their parents. It was never to be a permanent solution according to former President Obama, he called it a temporary solution until the Congress could come up with a program and that was five years ago.

In 2014, the Court declared former President Barrack Obama had no power to grant DACA or Dreamer program to the children illegally brought into country because, immigration law falls under the powers of the Congress. Other source claimed no court granted an injunction on DACA, and it was on the extended part of it that was rejected, whatever it was, only the Congress could act on immigration not the presidency

It was necessary to note how that five years old controversial order of Democrat Former President Barrack Obama would affect a Republican President Donald J Trump's administration if he was able to stop or continue it after the six months he gave the Congress to either pass a law to make it legal or massive deportations of almost 800 thousand of the recipients already in the country before 2007.

Who were the recipients of DACA programs which former President Obama illegally forced on the nation with his executive order?

To be classified under this program, one must be under 16 years, and must have been in the country before 2007, a year before Obama became the President, they must be ready to learn to speak English, the applicants must also be crime free or with no criminal records, in addition, the applicants must be in a college with limited opportunity to work full time.

According to President Barrack Obama, it was not an amnesty to circumvent the legal immigration law even though it was with the guidelines on its implementations. it was renewable every two years.

DACA was done out of political hidden compassion of President Obama after he was unable to get the Republican Controlled Congress to agree with his immigration policy and he decided without the Congress to write a law on immigration which the Court rejected because only the Congress could write laws in America.

President Obama in 2008 had promised the Hispanic group he would address the program that favored them more than any race in America, which was why he got their votes twice in 2008 and 2012 presidential elections, and out of desperation in 2014 he did what he could to put a smile on the faces of the Hispanics after the Congress refused his immigration plans.

Were DACA recipients solely whites, blacks or Hispanics?

From the locations of the states deeply affected like Texas, California, Arizona, New Mexico, and Nebraska it could be right to classify them as mostly Hispanics, the major immigration problem group in the United States of America at least to the White Americans.

Why?

To enter the United States of America by other races, like Africans, Europeans and Asians, they would have to obtain a visa and they could only come into the country through Airports legally, meaning, only those who came legally with proper documentations and over stayed may be seen among the so-called Dreamers and they were very few or insignificant.

However, because of the proximity and geographical locations, it was not the same situation with the Hispanics.

Majority of them came by land, desert and roads mostly through illegal routes almost difficult to control or manage by Homeland Security Department and almost 95% of the Dreamers today were Hispanics which culturally do not believe in family planning of limited children.

Averagely, Hispanics believe in 6-8 children per family which in future could enlarge the population of a race seen as a major threat to the Whites, that may even reduce the Blacks to minority of the minority for a long time.

What percentage of almost one million of recipients of DACA or Dreamers were blacks or whites?

Probably 5% and very few of this insignificant percentage were even from Africa, the rest were either from the Middle East who came in through Canada.

How would almost one million beneficiaries of DACA affect all races in the country?

With explosive population of the Hispanics, it would change the country a lot, demographically, including English as official language of the country, as most the Cities in affected states were no longer taking English serious as lingua franca of the country, they may even be powerful in future to re-write the Constitution if they could get up to 50-60% of US population, they were about 25% now.

How would DACA in future affect the election process of the nation?

A lot, the election process was still a bit porous as many doubts the refusal of Democrat Party to a verifiable identification process to cover illegality or "fake voters" in the way President Trump described the process.

To vote in America, you have to be a citizen, at least that was what the law says, on paper, in all the states controlled by the Democrats, DACA recipients were getting Driver's License and benefits like regular citizens and it was almost difficult to differentiate their immigration status from those of citizens, and if they were even voting, it could be the fear of the Republican Party as to the reason why the Democrats refused to grant verifiable voters identification that would tie citizenship with records in most of the states they controlled.

Was DACA done to benefit the Democrats Party or just the compassionate goodwill of President Obama?

Both could be the reason, because it was more like a welfare program, Democrats stands to gain more than Republican Party, meaning if eventually, DACA recipients were citizens with rights to vote and it was even a faster way to push the Whites more into minority group.

It was not a surprise, hours after Attorney General Jeff Session announced the plan to abolish the program former President Obama out of office called the action of Trump administration to stop the program cruel and inhuman.

The first noticeable problem of DACA started in the State of California with 55 Electoral votes when it started issuing Driver's license and all benefits of citizens to Dreamers, including tuition regulation like the citizens of Americans. In the state of Arizona, it was not the same when Dreamers were denied Driver's license and same tuition fee like citizens.

It became a legal issue that was challenged in the Court until the Court ruled DACA recipients were not regular Americans and as such, cannot be treated as such unlike what Obama policy was doing through the back doors.

DACA program became an issue in 2016 presidential election, the Democrat VP candidate Senator Tim Kaine openly campaigned in Spanish language to the discomfort of Whites America.

Tim Kaine the VP pick of Hillary was an afterthought, Castro from San Antonio in South Texas with ties to Cuba, then Obama's Housing Secretary was the suspected VP candidate since 2008 and why Hillary picked Senator Tim Kaine was a surprise probably out of fear to strike a balance between the Hispanic group and the Whites, it could be the only reason Senator Tim Kaine who could speak Spanish was considered, whatever, it was, it did not fly as she lost the election.

President Trump instead of kicking the DACA recipients out of the country as he campaigned, he asked the Congress to pass the law to either make it legal or all the so-called Dreamers would have to go back home, home to where?

It was the question on the lips of all and his political adversaries on the social media and mainstream media, like CNN, New York Times, Washington Post and Morning Joe a former Republican on MSNBC who changed his Party to Independent.

Joe fell in love with Mika the daughter of President Carter's late National Security Adviser Dr. Brzezinski, his co-host on the Morning Joe show, all of them called Trump names for keeping to the Constitution.

What would President Trump achieve from this after six months even first year?

The first part on DACA policy focused on the foundation and politics of DACA on ever changing immigration policies of the United States of America since President Reagan granted amnesty to millions of immigrants which eventually hurts his Republican Party as a conservative party of mean, and heartless followers of the Constitution line by line which did not embrace the welfare needs of the new immigrants, it was where the Democrats cashed in as a friend of the new immigrants.

The above little information on United States immigration problem happened before DACA and most of the past Presidents from Bush 41, who introduced Green Card Lottery to President Clinton who also signed the Life Act on the last days of his office, no other President addressed the so-called comprehensive immigration packages, they talked about. It was a no-go area.

Instead they picked on little pieces of it to appease different groups depending on what they could get from the Congress, meaning, what they told the people was not what they do behind the close doors. It was very deceitful.

After President Trump realized his Republican Party despite the majority in the Congress were not serious or he could end his presidency without a major Bill to his credit, he was now learning on how to talk and walk like a centrist politician, and to attain this, he took the first action towards moving his policies to the center when he hired General Kelly his Homeland Secretary as his Chief of Staff.

General Kelly

Almost all the far rightists in his White House were removed, from Priebus his first Chief of Staff, Steve Bannon his adviser on many issues to Dr. Gorki the Hungarian born adviser, it was when Donald J Trump made up his mind to change and dialogue with the adversaries, the Democrats particularly his fellow New Yorker and his friend Democrat Minority Leader Chuck Schumer, and the old horse in Congress Nancy Pelosi Minority Leader.

Blame his Republican Party, they were too petty, and disorganized to help his presidency and Trump realized the bucks stops on his table, not with John McCain who was still bitter because two years when Trump said he was not a hero, or his friend Senator Graham of South Carolina both could care less if Trump's presidency collapse like pack of cookies they were his enemies within his own Party.

To pass his Bills or to see some of his agendas before the hostile Democrats and careless Republican Controlled Congress, he had to make deals, and DACA became the first approach to a new centrist Presidency, it was a game Bill Clinton learnt in his second year in office when he hired Dick Morris, and Obama too did when he lost the House to the Republican Party.

In America, a Presidential candidate may campaign and win elections as a leftist or rightist, but to be successful he must govern as a centrist, if Trump must do anything in his first term he must walk the walk and talk the talk.

It was how the game of politics was played, far different from Real estate, hotels or golf course deals, it was not even a

Television reality show, it was a game of the heartless, controlled by the greedy special interests.

These were the options before the President who promised to drain the swam and may end up dinning with the very people he hated with passion.

To get things done on the wall he promised to build at the Southern borders, tax cuts and debt ceiling and approval/confirmation to his appointees he must compromise, it was the reason he did not ask the DACA recipients to go, and to stay away from the blame of the mainstream media, it was why he asked the Department of Justice to explain to Americans.

A new Trump would be strange to the Republicans like he struck a bargain on debt sealing few hours ago, he would get support on tax cuts and Trump wall, and GOP would reluctantly follow him.

Fifteen Blue Democrats states took the President of the United States of America to court over his decision to end DACA, which may be dismissed because Obama who ought to have followed the line of his predecessors on DACA, but he put it in writing which gave it an impression he was capable of writing immigration law, with that the case would be described as a waste of Court time, more also President Obama said the program would be temporary until the Congress could figure out something.

(40)

DACA 2

The President of the University of California Janet Napolitano sued President Trump's administration on his decision to rescind DACA. The school claimed the order to stop DACA would affect the students and lecturers in view of their meaningful contributions to the University.

University of California became the first to take legal action against the President to stop the program the Court in the past called illegal because former President Obama usurped the powers of the Congress with the program.

Interestingly, Janet Napolitano was the architect of the program for Obama in 2012 as Homeland Secretary. The case would come up in a Court with mostly liberal Judges and how the court would rule would be of interest to President Trump who hope to use the action as a bargaining power with the Congress over his Bills.

President Trump was pressured by 25 States Attorney Generals to act against DACA, however, all was not lost for DACA, which could still be renewed until October 5th, 2017, after that it would not accept new applications and by March 5th, 2018, the program would deem anyone not in compliance as out of status.

Some of the communities were aiding DACA recipients in California, including payment of $495 application fee or renewal fee, lawyers, and information on how to avoid confrontation with the law.

Furthermore, DACA recipients were not encouraged to travel out of the country or more than 100 miles outside their post according to Berkeley College information board.

(41)

Thinking like the British

When President Obama, a Democrat took over from former President Bush a Republican in Jan 2009, he rescinded all the executive orders of President Bush, and the former President George Bush never made a noise or formed a pressure group to make him unpopular with his actions, instead Bush kept his distance far away in Dallas Texas.

The above process had been the practice since 1789, when administration changes hand between two Political parties except if the government was between same party, no past Presidents since 1789 even shared Washington DC with a sitting President. It was called respect and understanding of the system of government, all these protocols Obama did not observe, or he would display complete ignorance of how the system works before him.

And it was shameful.

If President Trump rescinded all the executive orders of former President Obama, he would still be acting according to the Constitution of the United States. It must not be taken as personal unlike how Obama took it.

No administration was bound to keep any executive order of any past Presidents particularly, that of a different party, because of ideological differences and that should not be strange to any person except those with less attention to the details of US Constitution.

What was unethical and strange was for any past President to insist on making his predecessor to keep his policy in place years or months after leaving office.

If a past President was unable to have the Congress turn his policy into the law of the land, he must be wise and reasonable enough to understand as soon as he lives office, the next President other than the same political party with him may not share the same policy or idea behind any of his executive orders and it should not be taken personal when those orders were removed, more also, if he too in the past did the same to the President he succeeded, which was what happened to how he Obama rescinded Bush executive orders.

Furthermore, former President Obama was conducted his post office critics and pressure group against a sitting US President over his illegal orders could only show lack of understanding of US presidential system.

United States of America with her 1789 Constitution was not a British Parliamentary system, and there was no room for Opposition system hoping the government would collapse for his Democrat party to call for early elections. Or there would be room for him to have another term in office. It was never going to happen.

Another Democrats President Clinton in the pas said he wished the Constitution could be changed for him to run for third term, which was why he invested on his wife Hillary to run for office, he told the Press he just wanted to ride Air Force One again, which was the reason, this writer, in past wrote the Democrats have no respect for the Constitution of the country, the Party was too much of European thinking than the founding father's principles behind 1789 Constitution.

(42)

Paul John Manafort.

By the second phase of Trump's Campaign which faced increasing problems from the establishment within the Republican Party, it was time for Donald J Trump to learn the ugly rules of the American politics controlled by Clinton and Bush machineries since Ronald Reagan left in 1988.

Failure to change plan would make Trump to lose his delegates to Senator Ted Cruz Of Texas or Gov John Kasich of Ohio, which the rules of the Party gave the right to vote for another candidate if the candidate of their choice did not win on the first ballot at the Ohio convention.

It was that open system in the GOP regulation that kept Governor of Ohio John Kasich going hoping the front runner Donald J Trump would fail on first ballot, and it was for the same reason, Senator Ted Cruz kept the pressure on Trump, he saw in himself as the most conservative in the race, along with Gov John Kasich both were secretly cutting Trump's delegates for a switch.

Corey Lewandowsky, the young enterprising Campaign Manager who took Trump through the rough road from June 2015 to the early wins became the first casualty of what and how candidate Trump, despite his reservation caved in to the pressure of the Party if he had to win. Corey had to go.

It was a painful decision for both, Corey trusted Trump even when he fired him, his trust was not in doubt, CNN which hired him with the hope he would spill the beans on Trump was disappointed. Corey remembered how Trump stood by him when he was charged for battery over a false accusation from a lady who claimed she was attacked.

However, winning was everything to Trump, he applied his Television and Real Estate skills and talk to sway the American electorates, it was like they watched soap opera. He kept the nation and world glued to the Television, every day and every moment, at the GOP debate, his place was assured, he was the center of attraction.

If the event could be likened to a motor show, Trump would the most expensive red car on the lot, if it were a gun show he would be more than Ak47. Trump was going to win but if losing the delegates at the convention was glaring he had to do more.

The Bush families were going to support Hillary, they made it clear, Bush 43rd had given up on GOP, he said he might be the last GOP President, since his brother was defeated by the words of Donald Trump as a low energy candidate, he had made effort to prop up his brother dwindling political numbers in polls and it did not help, his mother too came, it was very sad when Jeb dropped out of the race.

President Obama the incumbent was going for Hillary, he was ready to play the Black vote card, he told African Americans he would consider it an insult if Trump became their choice, it was the first time a sitting President threw everything out to campaign for a candidate, at one stage Obama hugged Hillary with their eyes closed and one could see the helpless of President Obama in his ability to transmit his winning magic to Hillary.

Donald Trump was going to fight the war on his own against the two terms, of Bush, and one term of Bush Snr, his father and the Clinton political machines that had all the Blacks like that of Obama in the pocket and women too. It was a difficult task, Trump knew apart from winning, he had no choice because the other option was too mean and ugly to imagine.

The above became the reason Trump accepted the proposal to try the mafia of American politics. Paul John Manafort born on April 1st was not a fool, 1949 or so, he made kings, Emirs and presidents around the world, if it could be done, it must be Paul, the grandson of Italian Immigrant in 1907.

Grand pa Manafort had left Italy, the home of the Mafia for America to establish a construction company which he later changed the name to Manafort Brothers, his son, Paul and wife

Antoinette in 1949 gave birth to Paul John Manafort, who studied law and made a name for himself in politics.

Paul was the Meyer Laski of US politics, the political adviser to President Gerald Ford, President Ronald Reagan, And George Bush Senior, he made them winners, and he was the adviser to most controversial world leaders, in Europe, President Viktor Yamkorysh of Ukraine, Marco of Philippines, Mobutu Sese Seko of Congo, and Savinbi of Angola.

The few months, he stayed with Trump campaign team, he kept his promise, he kept the delegates for Trump and when the Russian old case came on Paul, he had to go.

How come FBI did not inform candidate Trump, his staff newly appointed Campaign Manager Paul Manafort for less than 4 months was under investigation since 2014 as required by the law?

And who was the FBI Director who looked the other way when Paul was hired?

It was James Comey.

Did FBI intentionally mislead Trump on or it was just an oversight?

James Comey did not provide any answer to it.

Who recommended Paul Manafort to Trump to hire before the 2016 convention? Are they not the e same establishment who did not want Trump to run as President?

These were the current investigations going on in attempt to clean up the FBI under Christopher Wray.

Paul pleaded not guilty to charges of money laundering and tax evasion 12 counts with Gates his deputy and both challenged to jurisdiction of the Special Counsel.

As deeply connected Paul was to Ukrainian politics and that of Russia almost a year into the Special Counsel investigations, no collusion had been established

(43)

Special Counsel

It became obvious, the Russian collusion was no longer what the public were made to think, it could be a plan B of the insider of the FBI and Obama administration based on the email found with the Andrew McCabe of the FBI and others by the Inspector General reviewing activities of the FBI and Department of Justice in the last eight years or so.

Just when President Trump was almost getting settled into his job as the Commander in-Chief and his inability to secure a better Attorney General than Jeff Session who was yet to shake off his Senate garment from being over too cautious to a risk taker, when he recuses himself from Russian collusion investigation, it opened the door for the anti-Trump in the FBI and Department of Justice to poke into his infant Presidency.

President Trump had just fired the Acting Attorney General Yates who refused to carry out the order or defend the newly inaugurated administration over the travel ban, and Jeff Session did not protect the infant administration either, the job of the DOJ fell into the hands of Rod J Rosenstein a new Deputy Attorney General who was confirmed DAG on April 26th, 2017 and his actions exposed the Trump administration to Special Counsel just like Janet Wood Reno who served as the Attorney General under President Clinton stupidly did in the nineties.

The investigation was planned and organized by the fired James Comey who leaked secret document through his friends to the Press, and by the time Robert Mueller a former FBI Director who reported to Comey in the past in the Department of Justice and who unsuccessfully interviewed for the FBI position was appointed the Special Counsel to investigate Trump, it was clearer he had to finish the job he started when he left office in 2012 for Comey which was his unfinished job of investigating Paul Manafort.

Paul Manafort decided to take the Special Counsel Mueller to court for exceeding the boundary of his job which was to find our any Russian collusion with Trump Campaign, almost a year into its assignment nobody had been found guilty of the primary intention of the investigation.

Deputy Attorney General, Rod J Rosenstein who appointed the Special Counsel and newly appointed FBI Director Christopher Wray both made spirited efforts to persuade Speaker Paul Ryan to cover the details of the document used as the foundation of the investigation which had inputs of Hillary Clinton and the dirty guys working for FBI and Department of Justice in it.

Unfortunately for the FBI and DOJ, Speaker Paul Ryan denied their request if FBI and DOJ had nothing to hide let it be opened which will be the only way to protect the system from the "Deep Red" the President mentioned.

(44)

Department of Justice

What could be very sad would be if all the allegations made on the deep red shit was found to be true, that inside the FBI and Department of Justice, a click of people very close to the White House operated like Mafia to pervert Justice particularly to protect Hillary Clinton and some of the messes created by President Barrack Obama.

When then Obama's Attorney General Lorretta Lynch directed the immigration Department grant visa waiver to a Russian Attorney to enter the United States of America at a time the opposition was campaigning vigorously could be link to the role the Russian Attorney played after her stay in the country was no longer necessary, It appeared now that the only reason the Russian lawyer, who might have pulled a bait-and-switch to get a meeting with Donald Trump, Jr., was granted entrance to the United States by Attorney General Loretta Lynch under a visa waiver program back in 2015 was part of the plan B expressed in the email of one of the FBI to MS Page that it was too risky to have Trump as the President of America.

The Hill News reported **The Russian lawyer who penetrated Donald Trump's inner circle was initially cleared into the United States by the Justice Department under "extraordinary circumstances" before she embarked on a lobbying campaign last year. that ensnared the president's eldest son, members of**

Congress, journalists and State Department officials, according to court and Justice Department documents and interviews.

And when the dossier used by FBI to spy of Candidate Trump Campaign team, it was obvious everything was teleguided from the White House, this revelation means, it was the Obama Justice Department that enabled the newest and most intriguing figure in the Russia-Trump investigation to enter the country without a visa.

Later, a series of events between an intermediary for the attorney and the Trump campaign ultimately led to the controversy surrounding the president's eldest son.

Just five days after meeting in June 2016 at Trump Tower with Donald Trump Jr., presidential son-in-law Jared Kushner and then Trump campaign chairman Paul Manafort, Moscow attorney Natalia Veselnitskaya showed up in Washington in the front row of a House Foreign Affairs Committee hearing on Russia policy, video footage of the hearing shows.

She also engaged in a pro-Russia lobbying campaign and attended an event at the Museum in Washington, D.C. where Russian supporters showed a movie that challenged the underpinnings of the U.S. human rights law known as the Magnitysky Act, which Russian leader Vladimir Putin has reviled and tried to reverse, the FBI Andrew Maccabee who planned to retire this year may be denied and all those who conspired to create the misleading dossier may all be prosecuted and it will be clear to imagine Hillary Clinton may find it difficult to escape the hand of the law this time around.